M000096701

STUDENT OWNERSHIP

STUDENT OWNERSHIP

Five Strands to Success for All Students

Lewis Willian and Rocky Wallace

ROWMAN & LITTLEFIELD
Lanham • Boulder • New York • London

Published by Rowman & Littlefield
A wholly owned subsidiary of
The Rowman & Littlefield Publishing Group, Inc.
4501 Forbes Boulevard, Suite 200, Lanham, Maryland 20706
www.rowman.com

Unit A, Whitacre Mews, 26-34 Stannary Street, London SE11 4AB

British Library Cataloguing in Publication Information Available

Library of Congress Cataloging-in-Publication Data Is Available

ISBN 978-1-4758-4315-6 (cloth: alk. paper)
ISBN 978-1-4758-4316-3 (pbk: alk. paper)
ISBN 978-1-4758-4317-0 (electronic)

♾™ The paper used in this publication meets the minimum requirements of
American National Standard for Information Sciences—Permanence of Paper
for Printed Library Materials, ANSI/NISO Z39.48-1992.

Printed in the United States of America

Contents

Preface

Many states are now using the percentage of college and career-ready graduates from a high school as a measure of that school's effectiveness. In order to increase the level of CCR, the schools often have tried drastic steps such as retraining the teachers, replacing the principal, retooling the curriculum, reorganizing the school day, and requesting additional help from parents. All of these are useful steps in improving student achievement. However, none of these steps specifically addresses the one individual who can have the most impact on a level of college and career readiness: *the student*.

Often, high school seniors take course after required course and test after standardized test without ever knowing *why*. Questions like: "Why does this test matter to me?" or "Will this test help me reach any goal in any way?" are on the minds of students. Interestingly, these same questions are often on the minds of the students' *teachers* as well.

Our hope is that this book will be a helpful resource in preparing high school students for successful transition to postsecondary life. Here, we walk the reader through a step-by-step process that transformed a school's college and career readiness model.

In an age that demands a well-trained workforce as never before and the matching of students with productive and fulfilling careers, it is no longer an option to leave postsecond-ary education to chance—with far too many of our high school graduates living beneath their potential. Great strides are being made in CCR that will positively impact students' future ways of life.

We have much to celebrate over the progress that has been made in recent years. But we're not there yet. There are still too many kids dropping out of school, still too many underedu-cated, and still too many not working at all. While we have them within our circle of influence, let's shepherd them to the finish line.

Acknowledgments

Many people are forced to look far and wide for a mentor to guide them along their chosen path, but my mentor found me when I enrolled in my doctorate program. Thanks, Rocky, for the knowledge, the understanding, the guidance, the correction, and the friendship. Thanks also to Dr. Michael Hylen and his department in the School of Education at Asbury University for your shared vision of what servant leadership should look like in schools that function well. Thanks to my family for your continual understanding and patience with me as I put this work together.

Mostly, thank you to the students, teachers, administrators, and the Lee County district and Kentucky Department of Education staff who partnered together to help the students in this school succeed—going from the bottom 5 percent in the state to the top 5 percent in transition readiness in two years. Each of you are the real heroes—this book just chronicles your journey.

—Lewis Willian

A special thank you to Dr. Tom Koerner and his Rowman & Littlefield team. Over the years, Tom has always provided professional and helpful support for the projects we have worked on together. He and his staff are a blessing and continue to touch countless others with their good work.

—Rocky Wallace

Introduction

This work is the result of two years of research within a rural high school in southeastern Kentucky. The strategies and activities contained within this work are an outgrowth of original research based on three fields of study: characteristics of *effective schools*, the impact of *student ownership* of their learning, and processes that lead to *sustained improvement* over time. When these three areas were reviewed in the literature, five common themes were identified that would drive a school culture improvement toward student ownership of college and career readiness, as shown in table 0.1.

These five themes became the focus (strands) of *Student Ownership*. When implemented in the case study school, this set of strategies and activities had significant impact on 1) the percentage of students who graduated college and/or career ready and 2) the teaching and learning culture within the school itself. The case study school (after implementing the strategies contained within *Student Ownership*) nearly tripled its college- and/or career-ready (CCR) score of 29 to a score of 81 in two years. These strategies have proven to be effective. Most importantly, students graduated from the case study school more productive and prepared for the next stage of their lives.

This work is designed within each of these five strands with two types of strategies: pieces to be completed with *student* and

1

Table 0.1. Common Characteristics for Student Ownership from Review of Literature

Focus Areas from Review of Literature			Five Common Themes (Student Ownership Strands)
Effective Schools Research	Student Ownership Research	Sustainability Research	
High expectations	High expectations for self	Goal-driven behaviors	**VISION** for improvement
	Empowered learning and self-responsibility	Persistence	Individual **OWNERSHIP** of the learning
Monitoring of progress	Self-awareness	Review and monitor for impact and individual self-monitoring of goals	Continuous **MONITORING** of progress toward goals
Time on learning tasks	Reflect on how individual students learn	Individual student capacity	**INTERVENTION** to help students meet goals
Clear mission	Celebrate personal and group successes	Relentless focus on success	**CELEBRATION** of student success

Source: Willian 2014.

other pieces to be completed with *teachers and administrators*. The end results of *Student Ownership* implementation are:

1. Increased percentage of students college/career ready
2. Improved student ownership
3. Improved school culture of professionals (for long-term sustainability of change)

A variety of strategies and activities are presented to help schools change to a culture of ownership for the students (and teachers). Each school will find something within this module to help students and adults focus on the goals of college and career readiness for all. When students "own" their learning, the focus falls onto success instead of failure. These steps and strands were closely tied with success in the case study school, and they will help you help your students focus on their own learning as well.

Understanding the Author's Perspective

The Power of Student Ownership

> This book is about what can happen in a classroom and
> within a school when students take ownership of their
> own learning and their individual academic results. These
> strategies flow from my real-life experiences in this area.

During the first fourteen years of my teaching career, I taught
science in a rural Kentucky high school. As with any beginning teacher in a large high school, I was assigned to teach the
classes that those teachers with seniority did not want to teach.
Fresh out of college, full of new ideas, I was handed a schedule
that said I was going to teach Basic Biology my first year. No
Advanced Placement or college prep biology courses for me—
but Basic Biology. The department head told me that those kids
"needed" me. She said "all of our new science teachers begin by
teaching Basic Biology." As she turned away from me, I'm pretty
sure she was laughing under her breath.

Basic Biology was for struggling students who had already
failed a "regular" biology course a couple of times. These students were way off track to graduate with their peers in four
years—the school administration was just trying to get them
a watered-down biology credit so they could somehow be
awarded the minimum credits required to finish high school.
The assigned textbook was a glorified coloring book. Veteran
teachers informed me that if I could just keep these kids from
killing each other or destroying school property, then I would

have a good first year. The expectations for any actual acquisition of knowledge by these students were nil.

So I followed the veteran teachers' advice. We did have an uneventful first year. We showed movies and we used our coloring book text. I'm not sure how much they learned. My students received their passing grades and they got their diplomas. By all accounts, on my first teacher evaluation I was a success. However, I'm quite sure that my students were not prepared to be successful (in scientific endeavors or in life in general).

At the end of that year as I reflected on that first teaching experience, I wasn't very satisfied with my career choice. I hadn't had much of an impact that year. I hadn't really changed lives. My students were a year older, but they really were not a year wiser. I was disappointed with the type of teacher I had been that year. I was certain I had wasted a year of my life. And I interviewed that summer at a local chemical plant to see if I wanted to change careers.

Luckily, I didn't change careers. Somewhere during the professional development of that summer between year one and year two, I started to get a glimmer of understanding of the role of expectations in student learning. I started to understand that if they didn't see the reason to learn the content then they weren't going to learn the content. I started researching the role of expectations in student engagement. In short, I started to think about how I could make Basic Biology less *basic*.

So before the second year started I went to my department head with a list of things I wanted to purchase for the Basic Biology class (for example, DNA model kits, dissection specimens, microscope slides). I received an answer from the department head of "No—we do not need to spend that kind of money on the Basic Biology class."

That answer did not sit well with me. In fact, it set me on fire inside. I started to wonder why these kids were less important. I started to wonder why some taxpayers' children weren't worth as much as other taxpayers' children. In that moment, I decided to do something about it.

My first step was to go to the old bus garage in the district where out-of-date textbooks go to lay and die. Out of the cobwebs, I dug out the set of old two-inch-thick dog-eared college prep books (at least two editions out of date) and hauled them back to the high school myself to use in this class. I backed my pickup truck up to the door of the science wing and began unloading those old books onto a handcart. I got some strange looks from my peers when I wheeled them into my classroom. I distinctly remember one of my peers rolling her eyes at me.

I then used what limited budget I had to purchase as many dissection specimens as I possibly could—and decided to teach Basic Biology as a comparative anatomy class. We traced the development of human systems through the animal family tree. We dissected, and we dissected, and we dissected some more. I had little cards printed and laminated that had the letters D.I.R.T. on them (Dissecting Investigative Research Team).

Students proudly carried these cards in their wallet and used them to enter school in the off hours to come to my lab. We stayed after school to dissect larger specimens. They began to see the connection between the earthworm's system and their own. They were mystified in finding the babies in a pregnant dogfish shark—and the discussions that were generated from these sessions were deep, specific, and lasting.

In the plant part of the year, students became plant specialists. Their leaf collection suddenly was not an exercise in "let's see how many leaves your mama and daddy can find for you," it was a true dendrological look at the differences in leaf specimens' vein patterns, how they functioned, and why they are the way they are. I decided to teach biology, not basic biology, regardless of what the schedule said I was supposed to teach.

Over time, something began to happen in these kids. I wish I could sit here and state that every child blossomed, that every child became a neurosurgeon or a rocket scientist. I wish that I could report that all of them are now living in huge houses with swimming pools. Unfortunately, that's not the case.

I did have students who went on to scientific careers—a veterinarian and a physician's assistant came out of that group. You see, once they learned that science was interesting—and that they could understand it if it were taught to them in a nonlecture class—then they found their success footing. These students told me later that our time together in the Basic Biology class was a positive turning point for them in their academic development.

That was an awesome thing to hear, but the point that must be made here is that the students did not change their attitude toward a success viewpoint until *after I did as their teacher*. My attitude impacted theirs. If I believed in them, then they knew it was permissible to believe in themselves. Success for all came down to the level of expectations I placed on them and the level of student ownership they accepted for their own academic work.

In order to change the teaching culture within the building, leaders must impact what teachers take responsibility for (that is, the curriculum and student learning) as well as what the students "own" (that is, their individual successes). This book is designed to help teachers take ownership of their students' learning. Through them, the students engage and own their personal academic path as well. The following pages contain strategy after strategy to help both students and teachers become prepared for the transition to college, the military, or directly into their career.

—Lewis Willian

What a joy to have the opportunity to collaborate on this project with Dr. Lewis Willian. I first met Lewis when I was at Morehead State University, and he was beginning his doctoral studies there. I was the instructor in his very first course, which ironically was on servant leadership. And now, he has masterfully utilized his research at MSU to author this powerful book that is definitely in the servant leadership camp—focused on effectively serving high school students in taking the time to mentor them into successful postsecondary education and career preparation.

Dr. Willian plays an intricate role in our School of Education at Asbury University. His versatility is a tremendous asset, as he develops and teaches a variety of courses, with his specialty being in the education leadership arena. He also helps recruit and mentor students for our graduate school administration program, covering the central and eastern sections of the state.

Most important, I admire Dr. Willian for how he lives his faith, loves his family, models innovative and scholarly work, and gives back to his church and community—a servant leader of the rarest kind, and a blessing to all who know him.

—Rocky Wallace

1

Establishing a VISION among Your Students

It's a Long Life

High school students are in a precarious position as they wrap up their last couple of years. Half child, half young adult—they are not experienced enough yet to understand life's harsh realities and how much weighs in the balance on the decisions they will be making in the next few months. Thus, they can tend to not pay attention to opportunities offered them at school or to college recruitment days, visits to local campuses, and info sessions on how to apply to schools and for scholarships.

Sadly, sometimes the high school itself is too understaffed to truly reach out to every upperclassman with the individual attention that is needed. And often, parents don't know the right questions to ask and the critical importance of aggressively helping out at home on the process of transition from high school to postsecondary.

It's a Long Life

When I was still a kid, but suddenly expected to be a grown-up, in a five-year span I basically made all the key decisions for the rest of my life. Whether to go after more education after high school, what school, what major, then marriage, securing a home, children. Honestly, I was barely able to microwave a meal. I would every now and then look at all the adult reality I was now faced with and say to myself, "Are you kidding me?"

Rick rushed home from school. He was late for his ride. Tommy "Tractor" Johnson had promised him part-time work over in the next county, and today was the first day.

"Where you rushing off to, Honey?" Rick's mom was cooking supper, and noticed he had not even stopped to give her a peck on the cheek when he burst through the door.

"Gotta run, Momma. Got me a job lined up for the rest of the spring. Could be permanent later on."

"What kinda job?"

"Repairing old cars. 'Tractor' says they need a new guy at this body shop where he hangs out a lot. Says if this works out, he may start up a used car dealership over in town, and he wants me to help him run it."

"Rick, I thought you were scheduled to visit the community college next week and talk to the head of the auto mechanics department. And I also remember you discussing the engineering program at the university. What happened to those plans?"

"Oh Momma. I'm not smart enough to work on an engineering degree. I talked to Henry Watson, and he said his brother dropped out after one semester from the same program I was going to look into."

"Is Henry your advisor?" Rick's mom's hands trembled as she tried to hide her frustration and heartbreak. All these years, she and Rick's dad had saved and saved—every penny they could—anticipating the day their oldest child would graduate from high school and chase his dreams. He would be the first in the family, on either side, to go to college.

"Now Mom, that's not fair. I tried to talk to our senior counselor, but it seems when I have a moment she's busy with other kids. After all, there's two hundred of us and only one of her."

"I thought she had called and scheduled a trip to the university for you. When did those plans change?"

"Well, actually, I forgot to tell you and Dad about that. You all were supposed to take me last Friday, but Dad had worked the night before, and you were running errands that day. I just figured it would be a wasted trip. I can't afford college anyway. I need to be out making money as soon as I can."

Rick's mom sat down in a chair at the kitchen table and could no longer hold back the tears.

"Honey, your father and I have been saving for years for this time in your life. Plus, there are scholarships and loans. Surely your school has told you about all of these programs that you might qualify for."

"Yeah, last year I think. But I didn't pay much attention. Too complicated. Besides Mom, I want to learn how to restore cars and make that my career."

"So just like that you're saying 'no' to the university? Not even so much as filling out an application, or at least a two-hour visit? We need to sit down and discuss this with your father when he gets home later tonight."

"Okay. But I'm not changing my mind."

"And you don't even think you need to go to the community college and learn this trade you have your mind set on?"

"Naw. 'Tractor' says I'll learn more by working on cars with this job, and then he wants me helping him with the car lot. Says we could make maybe $30,000 in the first year alone."

"Each? Not counting insurance and overhead?"

"No, not each. Come on Mom, it takes time to sell that many used cars. What's overhead?"

Rick's dad came in the front door, took off his ball cap, and went straight to the refrigerator to grab a piece of cold chicken from last evening's leftovers.

"Rick, tell your father what you've decided to do—without even discussing it with us." Rick's mom threw her head in her hands and sobbed.

As Rick, with the innocence of a kid and naive exuberance of a young man about to finish high school, explained to his dad about his job and his not needing any more school, the man who had put the food on the table the past twenty years and now was barely bringing in the money to raise four kids, looked out the window with a glazed look in his eyes. He felt broken and old. And he thought back to a younger time, when he and Rick's mother were getting married, and he badly needed a full-time job. So he had started driving a truck for a local company, just for a few months so he could make ends meet. He's still driving a truck—for the same company—after all these years.

"Son, it's a long life—when the shine wears off of that tiny paycheck and you realize this is what you're going to be doing with your life for the next forty or fifty years, day after day. It's a long, long life."

Questions for Reflection/Discussion:

1. Does your local high school have enough personnel and para-professionals to effectively handle the diverse needs of every student in the senior class as they transition on to postsecondary?
2. Does your local school district coordinate career days and regular student visits to postsecondary institutions?
3. Do you know a high school student whose parents most likely need assistance in helping their child in applying to various institutions of higher learning?

Specific Strategies to Establish a VISION in Students

Strategy 1: Initial College and Career Readiness Meeting—Explanation

Few high school students understand the difference between a "job" and a "career." If school can help students understand the lifetime earning potential difference between working for minimum wage and a living wage, students can grasp the need for advanced education beyond high school.

At my school, one of the first steps in impacting student ownership of learning and the need for additional education beyond high school was an assembly during which the vision was originally communicated. The focus of this meeting was "How can you be more successful in life?" and "How can we (the adults) help you reach your goals?"

Because of a lack of maturity or generational poverty, many students do not think about their future. As Ruby Payne says, they had no "future story." One idea to help students begin to see that academic success matters was to clarify their lifetime earning potential within a large group setting. This meeting kicked off a new approach to installing a college-ready culture within the school.

It was in this meeting that expectations for success are delivered and the importance of meeting the college- and career-ready benchmarks discussed. The focus was on *why* students want to meet the benchmarks to help their future earnings potential. It also focused on the fact that 70 percent of the jobs these students will be employed in have not been invented yet! An outline for this meeting's presentation/discussion included:

- Definition of "college ready"
- Definition of "career ready"
- Benchmarks and why they matter
  - Selection of senior course electives
  - Avoidance of extra remedial college courses for non-benchmark-meeting students
  - Graduating with honors
- Future income
  - A minimum wage job versus
  - A college or technical career salary
- Lifetime earnings potential
  - Specifically, how a college or technical degree increases a student's lifetime earnings potential
- Why this is important to *you* (students)
  - Why this is important to your bank account *now* (avoiding noncredit remedial college courses)
  - Why this is important to your bank account in the future (loans)
  - Why this is important to you as an adult (salary vs. minimum wage)
- Example of adult spending
  - Life with a salary versus life at minimum wage

This last bullet was the key point of the entire presentation. When the presenter clearly spelled out lifetime earning potential for a person at minimum wage versus a life at an average skilled trade or college degree career, the students were shocked.

For instance, the math on a lifetime of an hourly job might look like this:

- $10 per hour × 40-hour weeks × 52 weeks per year × 30 years = $624,000 before taxes

By comparison, the math on a typical career job might look like this:

- $55,000 per year × 30 years = $1,650,000 before taxes

Students may think at this point: "So what, both of those are a lot of money!" However, when you get to the next step, they change their mind:

- Subtract 25 percent taxes
- Subtract a $100,000 house
- Subtract 5 cars at $20,000 each (6 years per each car is a long time these days!)
- Subtract food: ($5 per meal for 30 years)
- Subtract insurance ($5,000 per year)

At this point, the minimum wage person was out of money and there are still several necessities of life that had not yet been purchased.

The information in this presentation surprised many students in the case study school. Student interviews conducted one year later indicated that this first assembly was an important moment in the initial formation of student ownership of their learning.

Strategy 2: Single-Page College/Career Readiness Flowchart—Explanation

Students are required to take numerous assessments throughout their high school career—achievement, skills, aptitude, career, or interest assessments are administered at scattered times throughout their school year. Often, students will take an assessment without knowing the value or importance to their future success. Some students take these assessments "because the teacher said I have to do so."

This visual artifact was used in conjunction with the student data notebooks to help students understand all of the requirements to be college and/or career ready—and the tests that helped meet the CCR requirements. Auditory learners were more likely to understand CCR from the initial assembly/explanation of why CCR is important. This piece was designed to help the visual learners "see" the path to college and career readiness.

This resource was designed to be an insert into the student data notebook as a quick reference sheet to guide their progress toward college and career readiness. It helped to demystify the process and helped students see what they had to do to be successful.

Because the requirements for college/career/military readiness vary from state to state and change across time, each state will have its own graphic that describes how a student becomes transition ready. The unique requirements of each state should be shared with all students to help the visual learners "see the path."

Strategy 3: Student Assignment to Transition Courses—Explanation

One of the most important pieces in establishing student ownership of the learning was the assignment of seniors who have not met the ACT college benchmarks to transition courses during their senior year. Seniors who had not met either the English or reading benchmark were assigned to a second language arts course (Reading for College Success), in addition to their mandatory English IV course. Students who had not met the math benchmark were assigned to an Algebra III course, which could also serve as their mandatory fourth math credit.

The assignment to this extra language arts class often dramatically impacted their senior schedule—meaning that the student had to give up a desired elective course in order to take the remedial/transition course. While not popular with seniors, this placement did have several desired effects:

- Increased the passion to pass the benchmarks (because the student could leave the transition course and return to his or her elective once the benchmark is met),
- Increased the desire to work through interventions (one on one and online) to grow in skill level,
- Increased the desire to retake the ACT or COMPASS exams and to try harder than before, and
- Increased the student's desire to make college visits and attempt to pass placement exams while there.

All of these were important pieces of students assuming ownership of their learning.

It was important that students understand very early that their enrollment in the transition course could be *temporary*. If the student met the missing benchmark(s), then they could immediately leave the transition course and move directly to their desired elective. Students exhibited (in the case study school) an increased desire to meet the benchmark and revise their schedule early in the school year, and this led to a significant increase in student focus and academic success.

It was also important to communicate this information related to senior transition courses for nonbenchmarkers to the *junior class* whenever possible, especially before the ACT was taken by students in March of their junior year. Students tried much harder once they had the knowledge that the results of that assessment would impact their senior schedule and potentially cause them not to be able to take desired courses.

According to adult ACT assessment proctors, this communication in the case study school caused the tested students to focus and give more effort on the assessment than in previous years. Data from the case study school suggests that the percentage of students meeting ACT benchmarks more than doubled (from 19 percent to 44 percent) in the first two years after transition courses were implemented. This was a strong incentive for students to focus on benchmarks and make the academic and assessment efforts necessary to meet these goals.

2

Establishing a VISION among Your Teachers

For Laci

> Life is not measured by length of days, possessions, fame, or position. In reality, one's life is measured by how we use the talents we have been blessed with to in unselfish ways make a difference in this world. This eternal truth separates the authentic servants from the pretenders.

As Jenny hung up the phone, she sat back in her chair and sobbed. Her niece had lost her life earlier that morning in an automobile accident. She was on her way back to campus—her dream was coming true. You see, Laci had been born with various physical handicaps. Although these maladies were a severe challenge most of the time, she had excelled in school and been accepted to the state university on a scholarship that she envisioned would eventually lead her to a career in nursing.

Jenny whispered a prayer for strength and kept her office door shut for a long time. As an elementary school principal, she realized she had to keep it together until her husband came by and accompanied her to her brother's house, where the family would be gathering. As she sat in a daze, her mind flooded with memories of Laci down through the years—birthdays, family get-togethers, special holiday traditions, summer vacation trips, sleepovers at her house with her kids—and Laci's endless thirst to be "normal" despite her physical frailty. She wanted no special treatment. She never complained about her problems.

17

She spent her time living her life for others and doing her best to reach her full potential.

Jenny returned to work the next morning and called a special staff meeting after school. As everyone filed into the library, many brought cards and hugs. And everyone cried as their "boss" allowed them to see inside at how much she was hurting. As Jenny began to wrap up the very emotional gathering, she asked everyone to stay a few minutes longer.

"Okay. I have an assignment for you—all of you. You see, my niece was a role model to so many, and certainly to me. As I have mourned these last two days, it has dawned on me that there is a gift I can give back that maybe I had not realized was right in front of my eyes all along."

Jenny stopped for a moment and looked around the room—making eye contact with everyone. "Now, I need you to write down a name of someone you know who is in high school that maybe is struggling with making a decision about college, military, vocational tech school, and so on. Maybe a kid from church. Maybe a neighbor down the street. Maybe a friend's child. Maybe a relative. Maybe your own kid."

"Now write down what you know about this student. Do both parents work? How many siblings? Hobbies? Both parents with college degrees? Or only one? Or neither? How much do you really know about this person who looks up to you and your insight? Or do you really know them much at all?"

Jenny waited for five minutes, then went on. "Listen to me. About half or more of the names you just wrote down—they will never make it after high school to where they need to be for further training that will lead to a fulfilling life. The high school staff can't keep up with such 'one to one' coaching and mentoring. It's impossible. And the parents often don't know where to begin."

"But you know these kids. They look up to you. They will listen to you. They will go with you on a day trip to visit a college campus. Think back to when you were their age. I bet for the vast majority of you, there was an adult you trusted who helped push you out of the nest, so to speak. Maybe a teacher. Maybe a coach. Maybe a friend's parents."

"For me, it was Alice Silverton—an older lady who always brought cookies over to our house on Saturdays for us kids. A great neighbor to Mom and Dad. And when I was about half-way through high school, she started talking to Mom about my future. She brought it up a lot—to me too. I began to realize that it was time—time to be making serious plans about college. My first year on campus? She sent me cards and cookies all the time."

"Here's what I need you to do. It's simple. Make an appointment with the high school counseling department. Take the name of the kid you just wrote down and find out where he or she is at in his or her plans for after high school. If it's not all solid and definite, if there's an application that's not been completed yet, or a student that's been hedging and seems to not be sure what to do, or the parents have not been coming to the training sessions on high school to college and career . . . simply start talking to this child and his or her parents. And take him or her under your wing as a mentor and advocate for him or her to chase his or her dreams—to their full potential."

"Is this too difficult for anyone in this room to take on? Just one child? Can you do it? Can you become an advocate for the family in this whole process of life after high school?"

Heads nodded all over the room.

"Thank you. This will be our project for the rest of the year. We'll discuss often as part of our afterschool meetings. And why is my heart so passionate about this?"

A young teacher held up her hand. "For Laci."

Jenny smiled, with tears in her eyes. "Yes, for Laci."

Questions for Reflection/Discussion:

1. Does your community assist the high school in some way in providing orientation and support for seniors in preparing for postsecondary?
2. Who in your life missed out on the opportunity to go to college or other postsecondary, and no one at the time seemed to know the person was struggling with the decision?
3. Have you ever taken a high school junior or senior (other than your own children) on a visit to a college campus?

Specific Strategies to Establish a VISION in Teachers

Strategy 4: Initial Meeting with Teachers to Establish Vision—Explanation

> Where there is no vision, the people perish.
>
> —Proverbs 29:18

The case study school that inspired this work was at a very low point in its history when the strategies contained in *Student Ownership* were implemented. The school had been classified by the State Department of Education as "persistently low achieving," a label applied to the lowest performing schools in the state. Administrators had been removed. A three-member state external assistance educational recovery team had been assigned to work within the school every day. Student morale was low, and teacher morale was even lower.

The initial work involved developing a shared vision for student ownership of their learning. At first, staff just needed to talk about what they were seeing and what they were *feeling*. The PLA designation was a "kick in the teeth" to this school—and they were not happy with the state, the local board, the students, or themselves. Blame was pointed and plentiful. The problems facing the school were all the fault of "these kids."

Early meetings involved talking about 1) where they wanted to go as a school and 2) how they would define success for students. Quickly, teachers began to make comments such as, "These kids do not care" or "Our kids are different than in other places due to our poverty." The insinuation was that all of the school issues and problems were the *students' fault*.

After processing what teachers said, school leadership developed and shared three new nonnegotiable ideas that they wanted the teachers to embrace:

1. "The students are not broken."

This district does enroll students who have external barriers to their learning (such as poverty, lack of parental involvement, or other issues). However, the students in the case study school were not that dissimilar from students in other rural schools, and many of these schools were producing far stronger student achievement results. If the students in schools with similar demographics and needs were successful, why must our students fail?

2. "Regardless of what they may say, all students want to be successful."

Students who did not understand the definition of success often act out in other ways so that the teacher's focus was shifted from the fact that they are unsuccessful. Many behavior problems were lessened when the students understood the expectations, were engaged in the class, and experienced some level of success academically. Students who understood the definition of success and had seen exemplars of success in their classrooms were far more likely to find success. They could find it because they knew what it looked like.

3. "Early success leads to later success."

As soon as a student received positive feedback for a job well done, he or she was far more likely to repeat the actions that produced this success in the first place. Belligerent, uncooperative students were often an outgrowth of a frustrating sequence of failures within the class, leading them to a conclusion that there was no point in trying because they knew they were going to fail.

In the case study school, a newspaper article was used in this initial meeting to describe the impact of small early successes on long-term early success. The key point was that it is counterproductive for students to fail the first assignment of the year because that set up a failure culture in the classroom instead of a success culture. The desire for success was an important part of developing lasting student ownership of their own learning and their eventual level of success.

The article was distributed, read, and discussed for implications on student success during the teachers' meeting on the opening day to start the school year. Teachers were given time to reflect on the article and then share within peer groups a response or a reflection of their thoughts. After these rich peer discussions, individuals shared any new thoughts generated by this article, and schoolwide steps to generate early success for students were developed.

Strategy 5: Single-Page College/Career Readiness Flowchart—Explanation

This artifact (same artifact used with students earlier; see chapter 1) was also extremely important for use with staff early in the vision-setting process. Unless the school has intentionally trained the teachers about *how* a student becomes college and/ or career ready, teachers will not advise students accurately as they help them take ownership of their learning. For example, math teachers will not inherently understand three-course auto mechanics career pathways unless they have been shown how that career pathway works. Similarly, few welding teachers will be able to explain what the math ACT benchmark means in terms of college readiness unless they understand it themselves.

Too often, school leaders just assume all teachers in the building understand all aspects of a topic without explaining it fully. The variety of assessments and certifications that can lead to college and career readiness for students can be confusing if not intentionally clarified. This diagram and complete explanation helped all teachers in the building (regardless of their content area) speak the CCR language to students with one voice.

College Readiness

The simplest explanation is that COLLEGE readiness is most easily met by achieving the minimum American College Test benchmark scores in English (18), Math (19), and Reading (20). These benchmark scores do not have to be reached during a single ACT administration, but can reflect the best scores students achieve across multiple administrations of the test.

Students who do not reach these benchmarks on the ACT may meet equivalent scores on the ACT COMPASS or the KYOTE (Kentucky Online Testing) assessments administered at the school or at a college/university. Once the student meets all three of these benchmarks, he or she is "college ready" and does not require remedial noncredit-bearing courses (MAT 090 or ENG 095, for example) upon entering college. While the benchmarks required can vary from state to state, this is a common process for determining if a student is "college ready." Teachers/school leaders in each state should research and communicate their own unique college-ready qualifications so that every adult in the building can speak a common message to all students.

Career Readiness

In order to graduate CAREER ready, students in most states must demonstrate 1) an *academic* proficiency and 2) a certified/tested proficiency in a *technical* area of study. The *academic* proficiency is best met by meeting the college benchmarks outlined earlier. That is, if a student is college ready, he or she is also halfway to being career ready.

In addition to those academic assessments listed earlier, a student can meet the academic portion of career readiness by passing ACT's WorkKeys assessment or the Armed Services Vocational Aptitude Battery (ASVAB) test. All of the seniors in the case study school who have not already met benchmarks take each of these assessments. This "multiple measures" approach ensures that students have every opportunity for success.

The technical proficiency required for career readiness can be met by passing a technical proficiency test or by attaining an industry certification. After students complete a three-course pathway in a technical area, they are administered a Kentucky Occupational Skills Standards Assessment (KOSSA) test in their area.

At the case study school, three-course pathways leading to technical proficiency can be attained in Horticulture (agriculture courses), Pre-Engineering (industrial arts courses), Transportation (automotive courses), Health Services (nurse aide and medical courses), Construction (carpentry or electricity courses), or Administrative Support (business courses). Passing any KOSSA test at the end of a three-course pathway meets the technical requirement of career readiness.

The other way to meet the technical portion of career readiness is to attain an industry certification in your specialty technical area, often involving performance tasks as well as written tests over technical content. Case study school students can attain automotive ASE certificates, construction NCCER certificates, business IC3 certificates, and health services Nurse Aide certification. Any of these certifications, when combined with the academic component, make the student career ready as well.

Schools should develop a one-page handout that shows the requirements for CCR as a flowchart to help clarify how each test or measure fits into the overall CCR system. Students must understand why each of these tests is important *to them* if they are to take ownership of their future. In order to facilitate this understanding by students, teachers must also understand why each of these multiple measures is important so they can fully explain their significance to their students.

Strategy 6: The Box (a Mental Model)—Explanation

At first glance, this strategy may seem insignificant. Teachers have a multitude of responsibilities and tasks to fulfill and accomplish during the school day that require their constant attention. The addition of one more "mental model" to their work may seem small, but it is actually a significant piece of student ownership of their learning.

In the initial meeting with teachers at the beginning of the year, teachers were asked to visualize a "box" contained within the brains of all of their students. On the outside of the box, there was a prominent label. It read:

"Things That Are Important To Adults"

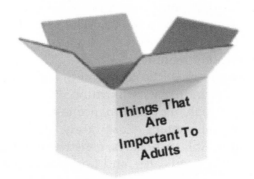

Teachers had to embrace this mental model and intentionally say and do things that made college and career readiness seem important. In this mental model, students (who want to grow up to be adults) were using their life and school experiences to constantly put things into and take things from this "box," storing away information related to things that adults *really* care about and focus their strength to achieve.

In order to transfer ownership of the learning to the students, it was essential that adult conversations and actions send a message that CCR was *important* to adults. If it was a consistent topic of conversation and a focus of classroom learning, then students would come to the realization that CCR *matters to adults*. When students realized that adults view CCR as worthy, valuable, and important, they began to place it in their brain "box" and value it themselves.

The case study school nearly tripled its CCR score (from a score of 29 to 81) in a two-year period. During the development of this work, graduates of the case study school were interviewed. One graduate that was enrolled during this increase in CCR was asked, "What was the reason CCR became important to you?" and "What happened to make students care?" His response, while smiling, was "Because the teachers never shut up about it!"

While humorous, this really was a significant response and insight into the students' minds. They heard the teachers continuously talk about the importance of CCR. The students began to understand this was important and took steps toward their adulthood because they believed it was important to adults.

This mental model was referenced in emails and in faculty meetings among the adults in the building. They were familiar with it and understood the important role it played in changing the school culture toward ownership of the learning by the students in the case study school. This too was important because it helped adults in the building put transitions readiness into their own "box" as well.

Strategy 7: Teachers as College Role Models—Explanation

Each teacher in the building overtly displayed his or her college credentials (including diplomas, awards, honors, or any other indicators of postsecondary study). Students were brought to a realization that each of their teachers successfully completed a college experience. It might have been easy for a student to forget that *all* teachers (even the vocational teachers) were successful college graduates.

An example is included of the type of doorside poster used in the case study school by every teacher. These posters were hung beside the door at student eye level of every classroom so that each student was forced to pass by these signs seven periods per day. They often initiated conversations among the teachers and the students about specific colleges attended and the pros and cons of each institution for that particular student.

This was a very easy, low-cost way to continuously promote a college-going culture within the building for all students. This strategy was implemented in schools at minimal cost and was a powerful way to help students develop their own "future story" and create a vision for their success when they left high school.

A sample is included.

Lewis Willian

Eastern Kentucky University
1985 BA Biology Education
1991 MA Biology Education
1993 Rank I Principal
Certification
2003 Supervisor of Instruction
Morehead State University
2014 Doctorate of Education
Leadership

My Family:
Wife **Carol**, Son **Matt**, Daughter-in-Law **Ashley**, Daughter **Julie**

3

Establishing OWNERSHIP among Your Students

Diamond in the Rough

> Every now and then, a person is born with a rare gift. It's as
> if they are put here on earth to be a blessing to others with
> this extraordinary talent—if given the chance.

Jensen was a quiet kid. Always had been. When his classmates were signing up for this club and that, getting excited about the prom, screaming loudly at a pep rally over one of their ball teams, well, Jensen just sort of eased into the background. None of this pomp and circumstance was his thing.

But in his father's workshop, in the basement of his parents' modest two-bedroom home, Jensen spent hours and hours with his passion. He loved tinkering with things. Simply put, he loved inventing.

In class at school, he had always turned his work in on time, complying with the rules of schooling and making good grades. But when he really got excited about learning was when he was exploring and researching on his own—on his intellectual level. By the time he was twelve, he had developed a prototype for a new type of bicycle that had a canopy for riding in the rain. His little brother thought it was so cool, but his parents had not a spare dime for anything, so he just left it over in the corner after a while.

When Jensen was fifteen, he was designing so many innovative projects that his father finally told him he had to stop. There was no more room in his shop for Jensen's "toys and junk."

At age seventeen, Jensen was given an aptitude test as part of his school's career readiness program. He blew the top off in the areas of science and mathematics. And a few weeks later, he scored a 33 on his first attempt at the ACT—the national exam that colleges heavily rely on for acceptance of graduating high school seniors into their programs. Jensen had always known he was a whiz at these types of assessments. But no one had spent much time talking to him about what it all meant in terms of his future.

Then Roy Hollins came along. Mr. Hollins was the high school's physics teacher, and when Jensen's ACT results came to his attention, he literally ran to the front office to find out who this kid was.

"Oh, that's Jensen," said the assistant principal as he gulped down a late lunch. "He's always acing these things. But his parents don't seem to show much interest when we reach out to them. I'll get around to making another contact this summer. You know, makes you wonder how these kids do as well as they do."

"I've never met Jensen. Is he on the academic team?"

"Nah, he pretty much stays to himself. We've invited him to take part in at least something that would get him more involved, but he tends to be a loner."

"May I talk to him?"

"Sure. I'll have him drop by your room after school."

Mr. Hollins scratched his head as he walked back down the hall and prepared for his fifth period class. "Who is this kid?" He thought to himself.

Jensen walked unassumingly to Mr. Hollins's room, wishing he could go on out to his old pickup truck and head on home. He had basically rebuilt it from scratch the summer before. And it was his hiding place every day as he drove to and from school. He loved the freedom of thinking about his projects at home as he drove.

"Jensen, son, who are you? Really, tell me about yourself . . . where you live . . . what your hobbies are . . . what your plans are for when you graduate from high school." Mr. Hollins had a way with kids, and he specialized in scouting and identifying hidden or dormant talent.

Jensen answered the questions quietly and had never had such an interview before. Before the conversation was over, he was agreeing to show Mr. Hollins his basement workshop on Saturday morning and had also agreed to join the school's Young Inventors Club, which met after school every Thursday. Mr. Hollins was the club's founder and sponsor. Jensen had been curious about the club a couple of times, but no one had encouraged him, so he had preferred to go home to his own inventions.

In the coming weeks, Mr. Hollins came to realize that he had stumbled on one of the most gifted students he had ever worked with. He was in shock. How had this kid not been discovered years earlier?

"Oh, Roy. We've noticed him. But he is a loner. We just figured sometime next year we'd land him a nice scholarship somewhere. But you know, his parents have to step up a little bit too." The district assessment director seemed to have experienced this before with other students. She wasn't alarmed or excited. It was just routine conversation as Mr. Hollins went on and on about Jensen and his talent.

Mr. Hollins was pleasantly surprised a month later when Jensen's parents showed up at the state showcase for young inventors. He had invited them but doubted they would make the three-hour drive. "So you think my son has potential, huh?" Jensen's dad was sincere as he sat down at the booth while his wife took a tour around the convention center floor with her son.

"Sir, I think your boy could be working at NASA someday, or pretty much anywhere else his heart leads him. But the next step is to get him into the right school—somewhere where the right mentors will take him under their wings and make sure he realizes how good he is with anything that has to do with science, math, engineering, physics . . . how gifted he is."

Jensen's dad smiled and looked off in the distance. "You know, he gets his curiosity for making things from his granddad.

My pop could draw anything, and he could turn those drawings into practical tools and such I'd never seen before."

"What college did he attend?"

"Oh, he never went to college. In fact, none of us have—on either side of the family. Jensen would be the first. Just never was a priority 'cause we've all been too busy working and raising our kids."

"I understand. But you do realize how much Jensen needs to go on to more education? The types of jobs he will be qualified for, they all will require a minimum of a master's degree—many of them a doctorate."

"Yeah, I do. His mother and I have noticed all along that school came so easy for him, he was bored most of the time. If you can find a place where he will be challenged, and can dive into it, we're all for that."

Mr. Hollins couldn't let this moment go by without pressing the point further. "What if I scheduled a visit for Jensen, and also you and your wife, to one of the top universities in the country? If I could somehow find some funds to help pay for the trip, would you go?"

Jensen's dad looked down and slid his shoe back and forth across the floor. "Sure, we'll go. Do you really think he has a chance at one of those bigshot schools?"

Mr. Hollins smiled. "I know he does. He's a diamond in the rough."

Questions for Reflection/Discussion:

1. Do you know a student in your community who has been blessed with unusual talent in a discipline that is not given much attention?
2. What does your local school system do to emphasize innovation and creativity in the classroom setting?
3. How are students in your local school district systemically provided visits to various colleges, universities, and other postsecondary schools throughout their middle and high school years?

Specific Strategies to Establish OWNERSHIP in Students

Strategy 8: Developing a "Future Story": Ownership of a Plan for College and Career Readiness at the Student Level—Explanation

Within the first month of the senior year, it was important for each graduating student to have a specific conversation with a mentoring adult within the school about the student's plan for the first year after high school—what they planned for their "next step" in life. For some, it was enrollment in college, others straight to the workforce, and some enlisted in the military. Each student needed to have a specific "Future Story" (Payne 1998) that helped him or her focus on completion of high school and led him or her to this next step successfully.

In our "Future Story" mentor-student conferences, we discussed each student's current status regarding his or her graduation, college and career readiness, and battery of senior assessments. The mentor came to each conference with the following data available: student transcripts prior to senior year, senior schedule, and status on ACT benchmarks in English, math, and reading. Prior to the conferences, the mentor studied each student's attainment of benchmarks and completion of three-course vocational pathways during his or her high school career to determine the areas in which the student could become career ready by taking a career assessment (KOSSA) or by attaining an industry certificate.

The desired outcome for these mentor-senior conferences was increased student ownership of the processes that would make the student college or career ready. The battery of questions asked by the mentor should be (will vary based on local factors):

- *"What do you plan to do immediately after high school?"* Answers will help lead to the focus questions for increased ownership of their future, discussed shortly.
- *"How are you doing on your ACT benchmarks? Which ones have you met? When are you planning to meet the other*

one(s)?" This makes the students think about *their* plan to meet *their* benchmarks. This is important for both college-ready and career-ready students (because meeting the college benchmarks automatically meets the academic half of career ready as well).

- *"Once you meet the other benchmarks and become college ready, have you thought about which elective class you want to choose?"* This helps them frame a goal of getting out of the transition senior English language arts course and into a preferred elective and helps them focus on why ELA success is important to them.
- *"Which three-course pathway(s) will you be able to test in for career readiness? Do you have more than one set of three technical courses in one area?"* These questions help students realize they are a specialist in something and that they will be tested in that/those area(s) at the end of the year to show career proficiency (which also increases ownership in their pathway). If they will be exiting a transition course during the year once they meet their benchmarks, discuss which elective will help them finish a three-course career pathway so they are eligible for an initial or additional career readiness assessment.
- *"What are you working on right now to help yourself become college and career ready?"* Remind students that all students who become both receive special honor cords to wear during graduation—this goal is very motivational for students!
- *"What can we do to help you reach your goals?"* This language puts the responsibility for student success on the students. It is an important piece of transferring ownership for success from the faculty to the individual student.

Each of these questions is designed to increase a student's ownership of his or her senior year success. These discussions helped to demystify the CCR process and give importance to the assessments the seniors take during their final year in school. When the students began to use language that states "I need to . . ." instead of "That teacher wants me to . . . ," then the students were beginning to own their learning and reach for the goals they established during these conferences.

Strategy 9: Student Ownership of Senior Year Course Schedule—Explanation

Throughout high school, students look forward to their senior year. However, students who do not meet ACT benchmarks were required by the State Department of Education to enroll in an additional "transition" English/reading course and/or enroll in a math course with extra intervention embedded during their senior year. These courses in reading and math are state-required interventions to help students become college (and career) ready.

At most schools, the reading transition course is a stand-alone full-year course, a "second English class" that all students who have not met their reading or English ACT benchmark must take during their senior year. This additional course often causes students to choose which elective course they will give up in order to take this required intervention course. In the case study school, this was not popular among the students. Students who have completed three years of study often look forward to flexibility and availability of open class periods during their senior year to take desired electives (now that their required core courses are completed).

However, this required additional English language arts benchmark class took the place of such a desired elective. (Math transitions could be delivered during regular math instruction and did not require a separate math course during the day.)

From a career-ready standpoint, this loss of an elective was also damaging to the students' three-course technical pathway completion. As stated before, in order to be career ready, a student must complete an approved course of study in a technical area with a minimum of three courses. This completion was negatively impacted if the number of elective courses is reduced by the need for additional intervention courses in order to meet benchmarks. Students needed the flexibility within their schedules to successfully navigate three technical courses in order to be eligible for career readiness.

So what was the impact of this knowledge on student ownership of their learning? Students were fully aware of the long-term consequences of failing to meet benchmarks by the end of their *freshman year* in high school so they could take early steps to avoid transition courses.

First of all, students needed to begin attempting the ACT exam early in their junior (or even sophomore) year. All students in the case study school were administered a state-sponsored full ACT exam in March of their junior year. If students met all three benchmarks on this assessment, then they avoided transition courses during their senior year. However, if they missed a benchmark, they needed to take advantage of the opportunity to meet the mark on any other regular Saturday administration of the ACT (which is given six times a year). Remember, they do not have to meet all three benchmarks during *one* test administration, they just need to meet the mark in each area at some point during their ACT career).

The impact *upon the student* of missing the benchmarks was fully explained to all juniors (and sophomores) multiple times during the school year. The school (teachers, administrators, counselors) intentionally communicated these potential negative impacts to all students:

- The need for transitional courses, thus taking away senior electives they desire.
- The cost of remedial courses in college that are required for nonbenchmark students (tuition charges but bear no credit, often delaying and dramatically increasing the cost of college graduation).
- The impact on completion of a technical career-ready pathway because a three-course pathway cannot be fully completed.

This was approached in a positive spirit (flexible schedule, cost savings in college) in order for students to continue trying to meet the mark. Students should "own" this process and be able to voice why meeting benchmarks matters *to them*.

However, if a student did not meet the benchmark by their senior year and had to take an English/reading intervention transition course, there were still ways to motivate the student to continue attempting to meet the standard. In the case study school, teachers continuously reminded the transition-enrolled students that they can exit the course once they met the benchmark. Often, students would attempt the very next ACT administration (at the beginning of the year, usually September) in an effort to move from the transition course. If they were successful, the counselor changed their schedule and moved them to the desired elective.

This was a powerful incentive for the student to keep trying. Students often took college days to visit local universities and attempted to meet the benchmarks while on campus by taking ACT's COMPASS computerized assessment. If the student passed, he or she returned to school with a printout that indicated the benchmark was met. The student's schedule was then immediately changed. Although a senior was only allowed two college days by school policy, the case study school permitted additional college days if a student wanted to visit a campus for the purpose of COMPASS testing. Several students took advantage of this opportunity to meet their benchmarks in this university setting.

Strategy 10: Student-Led Conferences—Explanation

Another significant piece of student ownership was the implementation of the student-led conference. Within this structure, students and parents engaged each other in a guided discussion about the student's strengths and opportunities for improvement. The student was provided ample support to prepare for and lead a discussion of their progress based on data from their student data notebook.

This work was divided into three parts (please see conference template).

Part A: Student-Led Preconference Goal Setting

Before the conference with their parents, students reflected on their strengths, weaknesses, and goals. Suggestions for growth areas for inclusion in possible goals were included.

Part B: Student-Led Conference Agenda

This agenda included the tasks to be completed during the meeting and included several "General Discussion Topic" samples the students could use to generate conversation about their progress and their needs.

Part C: Parent Comment Form

This template was designed for the parents to reflect on the student-led conference. It was left behind with the school in order to facilitate the students' continuing growth process. It also gave the parents the opportunity to reflect on and ask further questions that may have been raised from the student-led conference discussions.

Student-Led Conference Template
Part A: Student-Led Preconference Goal Setting

Table 3.1.

	Class: _____
My strengths in this class are:	
Things I need to work on in this class:	
My goals for this class:	

Goal Setting: Think about these topics and create at least two goals for this class in the space above that address some of these topics listed below:

- *Respect*
- *Determination*
- *Conquering your fears*
- *Responsibility*
- *Setting priorities*
- *Minimizing excuses*
- *Educational ownership*
- *Making better decisions*
- *Taking action on your dreams*
- *Developing a positive attitude*

Part B: Student-Led Conference Agenda

Name: _____

A. Talk with your parents about school in general. You may use the General Discussion Topics provided below:

B. Review the Student-Led Conference Form and your work from class (which should be in your Student Data Notebooks).

C. Close the conference.

- Have your parent complete the Parent Comment Form.
- Turn in the Parent Comment Form before you leave.

General Discussion Topics

School Behavior

- Do I pay attention and stay on task?
- Do I respect the adults at school?
- Do I always keep necessary materials and supplies with me?

School Citizenship

- How well do I get along with others?
- How do I treat school property?
- Do I follow school rules?
- Can people count on me to do my share of group work?

Study Skills

- Do I use my time wisely at school?
- Do I use my time wisely at home?
- Do I keep my agenda up to date and accurate?
- Is my daily work prepared on time and according to directions?

One way my parents could help me with school is:

Part C: Parent Comment Form

Name: _____ Student's Name: _____

1. What did you learn during this student-led conference?

2. What made you feel proud?

3. I would like to have my child work on

4. I am glad to see my child is working on

5. Any other comments?

Thank you for your participation and support of your child!
Please turn this form in as you leave so we can continue to help your
child succeed!

4

Establishing OWNERSHIP among Your Teachers

Someday

Too often, a student falls through the cracks at a major intersection of his or her life—graduation from high school. After years of preparation for this "moment in time," somehow he or she loses focus, puts off taking the all-important next step, or an untimely event turns his or her world upside-down. As a result, he or she begins a downward spiral that can lead to unfulfilled dreams and a life of regret. "What I could have done?" "What might have been?" "If I would have only . . ."

These laments of regret can be prevented—sometimes if just one person will notice and take the time to reach out a hand of support. Success is not a solo sport. Fulfilled dreams and effective lives are built on the shoulders of those special mentors—often unnoticed—who stand in the gap, helping lead the lost lamb toward home.

> Someday
> The saddest people of all are those who realize later
> that they let a mistake keep them from forging on with a
> relentless pursuit to reach their full potential.

Susan sat in disbelief. She could not focus on what the doctor had just told her. Her head was spinning and her thought processes became surreal, as if she was in a slow-motion movie.

"Brad, I'm pregnant." As Susan got in the car, her boyfriend of two years hit the steering wheel so hard his hand went numb.

"What do you mean, you're pregnant? I thought you were using birth control!"

"I have been. . . . Brad, I promise, I have been using it just as the directions say to for over a year now." Susan slumped in the front seat as tears rolled down her cheeks. And as she looked out the window, she realized her life had just changed forever.

"Well, we'll fix it, Susie. No worries—I have some savings. We'll end this mistake. . . . I know a friend who knows just who to hook us up with."

"No abortion."

"Come on, Babe. Don't start that religious crap on me!"

"No abortion, Brad! I'm carrying our child inside of me. Don't you get it? This is real life, you self-centered jerk! Now take me home. We can discuss this more tomorrow."

But there really was no more tomorrow for Brad and Susan. As the fall of their senior year rolled along into winter and then spring, Brad found a way to end the relationship as gracefully as he could, and Susan had her baby a week after graduation. She had been homebound for the last couple of months, not wanting to embarrass her parents more than she already had. And as the summer unfolded, she resigned herself to the fact that she could not possibly begin her freshman year of college. Her dream of being a teacher would have to be put on hold. But then one morning she heard a knock at the door.

"Susan? Hey there, girl. I hate to intrude, but I've been doing some last minute work for my seniors scheduled to start college this fall, and you were on my list. May I come in?"

Susan was surprised to see her high school counselor, Mrs. Hopkins, and enjoyed showing off her precious little one. But after the initial greeting and catching up, her mouth dropped open, as she couldn't believe what she was hearing.

"You what? Have found me a scholarship? To where?"

"Well, this small college about an hour from here. . . . You know, we discussed it briefly last year. A real nice school with a highly respected education department. Anyway, I was chatting on the phone to someone in their admissions office yesterday, and she mentioned an unclaimed scholarship for single moms that she needed to award as soon as possible. The deadline for admission to fall term is in two weeks. Are you interested?"

"What? How did I . . .? When did . . .? There has to be some kind of mistake."

"No, no, honey. Your ACT scores are in great shape. And there is a daycare there for your baby when she gets a little older. And it's not that long a drive. Could you find childcare for a year or so?"

"Well, sure. Mom would love to do that. She and I were talking the other day about me maybe finding part-time work so I could start rebuilding my life. But I just never dreamed there was a chance I could still go to college. I thought I had thrown all that away."

"No, you did not. It's right there for you to take and run with it. But we'll need to get your paperwork in real fast. You discuss all of this with your parents and I'll call you in the morning."

"Thank you, Mrs. Hopkins! Thank you, thank you!" Susan was laughing and crying at the same time.

"Congratulations, Susan. You were always one of my most promising students. Proud of you, kid."

Questions for Reflection/Discussion:

1. Can you recall a time in your own life journey when someone cared enough to stand in the gap for you while you were recovering from a setback?
2. Did you have a mentor that provided support and wise counsel as you were making your transition from high school?
3. Do you know a high school student who needs guidance and an extra boost of support or accountability right now?

Specific Strategies to Establish OWNERSHIP in Teachers

Strategy 11: 1:1 Mentoring Relationships with Students—Explanation

Many commercial advisory programs are available to help develop a culture within the school in which the adults mentor and advise the students. Many produce artificial group structures in which "activities" are completed to "build rapport" with the students. In some cases, this process works and a student develops a close mentoring relationship with his or her advising teacher. However, this is not always the case.

The question that should be asked here is: Why are we trying to force a relationship between an adult and a student who may not have common interests? Why not build upon authentic connections that *already exist*?

Think about it. The basketball coach is already connected to his or her players, as is the band director or the FBLA teacher. The FCA sponsor has relationships with his or her club members, and the beloved social studies teacher always has students hanging around after his or her class to talk for a few extra minutes.

Why not exploit those natural, organic relationships instead of trying to force artificial new ones?

At an early in the year faculty meeting at the case study school, each teacher received a list of every student enrolled in the school. Each teacher was instructed to initial beside the name of every student that they saw on the list that they had a preexisting relationship with—former student, current coach, fellow church member, child of adult friends, etc. The teachers were instructed to initial beside students who would come to them if they needed to talk to someone about their parents, their grades, or which type of car they want to buy— an authentic mentor.

After the lists were collected, a staff member worked through all of the teachers' responses and produced a matrix of *which student* was connected to *which teacher*. Some teachers were connected to multiple students, some to only a few. Each teacher was given a list of their authentically connected students to mentor. In the case study school, approximately 90 percent of all students were identified as having an authentic connection to a teacher during the initial survey. This list of connected students really did not add any extra work to the teacher—these relationships with students *already existed*.

What about the other 10 percent? The important finding during this process was the list of students who were not connected to *any* teacher. These were those students prone to "slip through the cracks" and struggle in silence. These students needed to have an intentional *forced* mentoring relationship with an adult in order to connect them to someone within the school.

This narrowed list of unconnected students was brought to the next faculty meeting session and a similar process was followed. This time, the teachers were looking for students they could force a connection with—students who were now in their classes, whose lockers were near their classrooms, or who they saw during lunch. Additional matrix work assigned one or two new unconnected students to each teacher so that *no student stood alone*. Each teacher was tasked with finding ways to talk with each newly assigned student and to develop a relationship where none existed before. This took work, but it was fruitful work. A connected student is far more likely to have a favorable outlook on his or her school and learning.

Once connections were set, teachers regularly talked with their students—especially if they were struggling academically. Grade reports were printed out at each midterm and end of quarter (eight times per year) and distributed to the connected teachers of struggling students. Assistance was offered or the student was guided to the right tutor to help him or her succeed.

This method of identifying and utilizing authentic relationships seemed to work better than artificial advisor/advisee programs. It was very intentional and very individualized. It led to trust-filled student-teacher one-on-one relationships that promoted student achievement. Students naturally gravitated toward specific adults that they trust and like. These relationships should be the basis for teacher-student mentoring work within the school. However, when a student did not choose an adult to connect to, the school chose the adult for him or her. The student did not know that he or she was "assigned" a mentor, he or she only knew that an adult in the building was showing extra academic interest in him or her.

Strategy 12: Let the Data Speak—Explanation

So far, this work has focused primarily on ways to get the students involved with ownership of their learning results. It was also extremely important to develop processes whereby *teachers* took ownership of their students and their learning results as well.

In the case study school, teachers initially offered myriad excuses to explain their students' (as well as their own) failures. Comments like "No one could teach these kids" and "I'm teaching it—they're just not trying" were commonly heard within the building. Expectations were low for students and they were consistently meeting those low expectations.

A key phase in the case study school's turnaround began once the school staff started examining student performance data on a consistent basis throughout the school year. Traditionally, teachers had looked at test scores once a year during a single-day "data review" and then made the disparaging comments listed earlier. The next year, when data review day arrived again, nothing had changed except for a rise in the teachers' dissatisfaction and frustration levels.

Anthony Muhammad discusses in *Transforming School Culture* (2009) a key step in the school improvement process. It occurs the moment when teachers begin to focus on *student outcomes* instead of the *intention* of the teachers.

In the case study school, true turnaround began when school performance data were examined as they were collected—throughout the year—by teachers, administrators, and *students*. Progress related to the benchmarking process on the ACT was measured six times per year, as the data were returned to the school after each test administration.

ThinkLink formative data was examined after each of the three test windows—each twelve weeks apart. Student progress (as measured by grades) was examined at each midterm and at the end of each nine-week grading period. Attendance data were examined monthly. Behavioral referrals were tabulated by infraction type and discussed four times per year. Data became an ongoing measure of effectiveness instead of a dreaded review once per year.

The artifact shown here was presented to the staff at every Tuesday faculty meeting to keep a consistent and constant focus on student performance and success. In fact, over time, the staff began asking for their "data sheet" if school leaders failed to have it available when the meeting started.

By the midpoint of the year, this data sheet was simply printed and laid out on the library tables at the onset of each faculty meeting, and the staff would have discussions about the data on their own during the gathering time before the meeting actually started. The staff began to see the data as something that belonged to *them* as the teachers in the building. These particular data points were selected because they all combine to produce an accountability score in the case study school's state (Kentucky). These numbers indicate the health and wellness of the school—their "vital signs" of health.

Another significant impact of this continuous loop of data was that these numbers become demystified over time. When data review was a once-per-year event, a great deal of time was spent on reteaching the meaning and usefulness of each assessment and test score. However, with continuous use, the data became relevant and understandable for all teachers and students. Teachers began to anticipate data jumps in *their* data and the administration made sure to point these successes out to the faculty at large. These celebrations of small victories made the staff hungry for more—they wanted to see the formative and intermediate data measures trending upward. This data became *their* data and they began to believe it actually mattered.

LEE COUNTY HIGH SCHOOL - DATA SUMMARY - End of Year 2012-13				
*indicates current data (5/13/2013)				

1) END OF COURSE ASSESSMENTS

	11/12 MC Avg	11/12 P/D%	12/13 MC Avg	12/13 P/D %
ENG I	153.3	N/A	152.7	N/A
ENG II	152.5	47.20%	152.6	43.50%
ALG I	143.9	N/A	142.5	N/A
GEOM	143.2	N/A	143.7	N/A
ALG II	145.1	35.00%	145.1	24.70%
BIO	148.4	25.00%	149.7	29.11%
US HIST	146.1	38.20%	146.4	54.02%

2) COLLEGE BENCHMARKS (ACT/Compass/KYOTE)

	11/12 Met All 3	11/12 %	12/13 Met All 3	12/13 %
Benchmarks	27/76	35.50%	38/83*	45.8%

3) WORKKEYS

	11/12 % Passed Before Retakes	11/12 % Passed After Retakes	12/13 % Passed Before Retakes	12/13 % Passed After Retakes
	39 of 76 (51.3%)	43 of 76 (56.5%)	52 of 83 (62.7%)	65 of 83 (78.3%)

4) KOSSA

	11/12 KOSSA Pass	11/12 %	12/13 KOSSA PASS	12/13 %
	22 of 77	28.57%	36 of 83	43.40%

5) INDUSTRY CERTIFICATES

	2011-2012	2012-2013
	12	29*

6) COLLEGE and/or CAREER READINESS

	College Ready	Career Ready	Non-Duplicated	Score (w/ Bonus)
2010-11	5 of 47 (10.6%)	10 of 47 (21.3%)	12 of 47 (25.5%)	29.0
2011-12	27 of 76 (35.5%)	26 of 76 (34.2%)	39 of 76 (51.3%)	62.5
2012-13	37 of 83 (44.6.0%)	45 of 83 (50.6%)*	52 of 83 (62.7%)*	81.3

7) OVERALL ACCOUNTABILITY

	2011-12	20%	2012-13	20%
Achievement	52.1	10.4		10.7
Gap	31.0	6.2		6.2
Growth	62.8	12.6		10.1
CCR	62.5	12.5	81.3	16.3
Graduation	68.6	13.7	91.3	18.3
TOTAL		55.4		61.5

Strategy 13: Constant Pressure/Changing the Conversation—Explanation

Another important piece of the teachers' facilitation of student ownership of the learning was for the conversation to consistently focus on college and career readiness. When we adhere to the mental model detailed earlier in this work that suggests that students judge the importance of a concept by the weight given to that concept by adults, it was essential that the adults talked about college and career readiness day by day and week by week. Students would take their cues regarding the importance of a topic based on what they heard (or overheard) adults discussing.

In order to facilitate this year-round focus on college and career readiness success, the suggested discussion topic calendar shown in table 4.1 might be useful.

Table 4.1.

Month	Discussion Topics to Keep the Focus on CCR/Student Ownership
August	Did you meet your benchmarks over the summer? Are you in a transition course? Did that change your schedule/impact your choices of electives? Are you traveling to a college campus to try to meet the benchmark(s) early so you can move to an elective you prefer?
September	Have you registered for the October ACT yet? Do you need to in order to meet your benchmarks? Do you need transportation or a fee waiver (for approved students of poverty)? How is your career pathway going? Are you sure you are completing a course of three technical area classes that will lead you to a chance at becoming career ready later in the year?
October	Are you ready for the ACT? Are you doing anything to prepare? Study materials/online prep? How is your career pathway going? Are you having any trouble? Are you looking over the career pathways standards so that you will be successful on your career assessments?
November	When will you take your industry certification assessments? How do you get ready for those? Will any of your courses be ending at midyear? Do you need to adjust your schedule for next semester to finish a tech pathway? Are you taking the ACT again in December?
December	Is your schedule set for January? Do you need to get any course or study materials ready over the break? Are you ready to try to college benchmark using the COMPASS or any other approved benchmarking test? Are you using any online tutorials (such as WinLearn, TCA, or Aleks) to help improve your skills? What can you do over the winter break to help you be more successful next semester? Have you applied to all of the schools that you are interested in? Do you need any help with that process?

(continued)

Table 4.1. (Continued)

Month	Discussion Topics to Keep the Focus on CCR/Student Ownership
January	*Are you taking the February ACT? Have you registered? What specific issues are you having that cause you to miss meeting the benchmark(s)? Have you looked at the ACT skills list for each content area and made sure you are familiar with everything listed there? How can we help you with that?*
February	*You're starting to approach the date(s) for your career readiness assessments and industry tests. How is your pathway going? How can we help? Are you continuing your online prep work? Are you working on sample questions from these assessments in class? What are you having trouble with? Are you using college visits to take benchmark COMPASS tests while on campus? Are all of your college admission requirements/paperwork forms completed and submitted?*
March	*Are you ready for all of your assessments? Do you need any last-minute tutoring on anything that confuses you? How can we help you be a better test taker? What do you need to be successful? Are you taking full advantage of all of the available assessments that meet some or all of the requirements for college and/or career readiness (for example, ASVAB, COMPASS, KYOTE, WorkKeys, KOSSA, etc.)?*
April	*How are all of your academic tests/career assessments going? How can we celebrate your successes with you? Did anything confuse you on your last test? Can we fix any misunderstandings and then offer you a retake? What other steps can you take to become college and career ready?*
May	*How can we celebrate your senior year with you? If needed, can we help you connect with the local postgraduate adult education center for more help? Even though you're graduating, in what areas do you still need to develop your skills to have a successful college or work experience? How can we help?*

This set of questions is not meant to be an exhaustive list, but merely samples of the type of conversation starters that can consistently be used to turn the student focus back to their learning and their level of college and career readiness throughout the year.

5

Establishing a MONITORING Method among Your Students

When We Fail to Plan, We Plan to Fail

I found an old "bucket list" recently—tucked away in a planner in my work desk at home. Had ten goals on it from about twenty years ago. I have accomplished all but one. Amazing how that works. . . . Write it down—it has a much better chance of becoming reality.

Melissa loved music. From the time she had been old enough to take piano lessons, she had explored the mysteries of how songs come to life, how music touches the soul, and how there are so many different genres of music. By middle school, she knew she wanted to pursue her passion for this art form seriously and was already thinking about what to focus on as a music major in college. But she had one main problem that was already haunting her: procrastination.

"Melissa, Honey, come on—let's go. You're going to be late for your first day of school."

"Coming Mom. We'll make it okay."

"Did you grab your flute?"

"Oh. No, I did not. Be right back."

Melissa's mom sat in the car and shook her head. Her patience was wearing thin. This child was a mess when it came to organizational skills. And it was beginning to hurt her in various ways. She had missed the deadline for a summer music camp back in the spring. She had forgotten to list her preferences for her schedule this coming school year back in the winter, thus missing out on taking both chorus and band. She had somehow lost a parent release form when her youth group at church was going on an overnight a couple of weeks back. So she missed the deadline on that opportunity too.

"Got it Mom. Thanks for reminding me. Would hate to miss band practice the first day of school!" Melissa chuckled, but her mom wasn't amused.

Melissa loved her life. She loved her family and all they were able to provide for her. She loved her friends at school and her studies—especially anything to do with her thirst for learning more about music. She had a promising future for sure.

But as her middle school years flew by and she began her high school experience, her lack of organization continued. And when she began noticing the boys more, even her practice time suffered. She lost her seat as first chair in the flute section in the band, and her piano teacher finally asked her to take a six-month break until she could get serious about the more difficult arrangements she was now capable of playing.

One evening, her dad peeked out over the evening paper he was digesting and asked, "Sis, everything okay? I signed your six-week report card, but wow, you took a dip in a couple of classes. Anything I can do to help?"

Melissa turned red, embarrassed. Her father was such a hero to her. She knew she had let her parents down these past few months. And it wasn't that she was dogging it. She simply did not know how to manage her time to get everything covered that was on her plate. High school sure was more complex than she had assumed. "Dad, I'm a typical flighty, 'head in the clouds' gal. I'll do better. I promise."

But as she got up from the couch to leave the room, her father calmly added, "I can help you with that, you know."

"Oh, come on, Dad, you've never been a girl. We just have so much drama in our lives, we appear to not have it together. But we usually do. Or at least I do."

"Really? I hope so, Sis. Tell me, how's your 'personal growth plan' going at school? I remember seeing that when you were a freshman last year, but haven't heard you say much about it."

"It's somewhere in my locker at school. Besides, we don't really do anything with it. Our faculty mentor asks us to bring it to her monthly sessions, but I usually just listen to the other kids and learn from the questions they ask her."

"Well, if I were you, I'd keep that handy and check off the tasks every semester that you are supposed to be completing or working on."

"What tasks?"

"Melissa? Come on. Did you even read it? Your school has outlined for you a clear and very doable path all the way through high school and successful entrance into college. If I remember, they have the semesters already identified for you to take various precollege assessments, when to begin visiting college campuses, when to begin sending applications to various schools, what tutoring is available all along the way. . . . Do you not take a glance at that plan at least every once in a while?"

Melissa looked down. "No."

"Okay, okay. Let's not keep spinning our wheels. Come over here. I want to show you something." As Melissa sat down on the floor by her father's recliner, he pulled out of his billfold a folded piece of paper.

"What do you see here?"

"Wow, Dad. You have a plan here for some terrific family trips in the next few years. . . . Are we really going to visit Canada next summer?"

"Yep. I call this my short-range bucket list. I have a long-range one too, but this one is what I'm going to help you with first."

Over the next hour, father and daughter together outlined a plan for Melissa's next three years. And at the bottom, Melissa signed that she would be the one responsible for staying focused on the goals or tasks and completing them. Her dad would simply ask her every three months if she was on schedule.

Seven years later, when Melissa had just earned her undergrad degree and was interviewing for her first position as a music teacher, out of nowhere came an answer to the question, "What are your aspirations for the next five years?"

"Oh, that's easy. I'm going right on to grad school, and also will be offering piano lessons at home for kids who are

interested. I hope to help this school grow the best music program in the state. I know this will be a lot of hard work, but we
can do it. My dad taught me a long time ago about how to set
goals and then work hard until they're achieved. His plan was
simple, and it changed my life."

Melissa landed the job and celebrated by booking her first trip
to Yellowstone National Park. You see, this too was on her "life
plan" short-term bucket list.

Questions for Reflection/Discussion:

1. Do you know a student in your community or in your own
   family who struggles with procrastination or poor time
   management?
2. What does your local school do to provide one-to-one support to students in life planning?
3. Is this support systemic and a well-designed plan? Does
   it include faculty/student mentoring and accountability
   checkpoints?

Specific Strategies to Establish MONITORING Methods in Students

Strategy 14: Student Data Notebook—Explanation

In order to create effective practices related to students' ownership of their learning, the student must first take ownership of his or her scholastic performance data. This piece was
designed to facilitate the creation of a student data notebook
that would be used by the student throughout his or her high
school career. This notebook continuously housed the latest
evidence (data and reflections) related to the student's level of
performance.

In the case study school, students kept two data notebooks—
one in their English/language arts course and another in their
math course. While our notebooks were housed in two-pocket
folders, some schools could have more expensive three-ring

binder systems. By the time the freshmen in the case study school reached their senior years, the volume of data was so great that they needed to transition from folders to larger binders.

Those notebooks were designed to promote ownership of the learning by the *students themselves*. Students received a copy of printouts from all of their battery of assessments—formative, interim, and summative. This data included the EXPLORE, PLAN, and ACT test results, their ThinkLink Discovery Ed results, and classroom assessment results from a variety of measures. As these data were added, explanations were delivered as to the meaning and significance of each new piece of data and what it told them about their learning.

To enhance ownership, the classroom assessment to student learning questions paraphrased from the work of Stiggins, Arter, Chappuis, and Chappuis (2006) were used.

Students were asked to respond to these three questions:

- *Where am I going?*
- *Where am I now?*
- *How can I close this gap?*

Students reflected on their progress in relation to these questions. In addition, students were taught to use a PDSA cycle (Plan, Do, Study, Act) to improve their performance and reflect on their progress and continuing learning needs.

The purpose of the student data notebook was to produce students who took responsibility for their own progress. This notebook was also very useful in student-led conferences as a tool for students to use when they explained their progress and goals to their parents.

Course: _____ Name: _____

Date: _____ PD: _____

Midterm Report Reflection and Goals

<u>Directions</u>: **Use your Midterm Report data to reflect on your progress thus far. Select and complete one item below that best represents your progress, thoughts, and goals.**

I) My Midterm Grade for the first nine weeks is _____.

(Select one item below and complete.)

_____ I am **pleased** with my current overall grade.

_____ I am **not pleased** with my current overall grade.

I earned my grade because: (Circle those that apply.)

- I completed all assignments.
- I met all due dates and deadlines.
- I came to class prepared to learn.
- I was prepared for class with all materials: paper, pen, book, etc.
- I participated actively and cooperatively during class activities.
- I used active study strategies to prepare for tests/quizzes.
- I kept my notebook organized.
- I was absent no more than two days for the marking period.
- I did not complete all assignments.
- I handed in work late or past the due date or deadline date.
- I was absent more than five times this marking period.
- I was frequently unprepared with my assignments.
- I did not contribute in a positive way to class activities.
- I did not use active strategies to prepare for tests and quizzes.
- I did not come with pens, pencils, or paper *every* day.
- I did not take responsibility for my own learning.
- Other: _____

I, _____ (name), plan to earn a grade of _____ in _____ (course) by the end of the first nine weeks.

The **actions I plan to take** in order to obtain my goals are:

-
-
-
-
-

Remember, only I can make a difference in my grade. With hard work, determination, and commitment, I can meet my goal and be highly successful.

Student signature: _____

"Actions" Ideas:

- Attend class every day.
- Complete all homework every day.
- Have all materials ready to begin class on time.
- Complete all classwork on time.
- Pay attention and actively listen.
- Ask questions in class to seek clarification.
- Actively engage in the lesson.
- Follow written and oral directions.
- Copy all information and show all work as directed.
- Seek answer accuracy on all assignments.
- Seek help from peers, parents, friends.
- Maintain an organized binder with all materials, assignments, resources, notes, etc.
- Accurately copy all assignments and check assignment book each night.
- Make up all work on time.
- Utilize every opportunity to retake English/reading assessments, ACT, COMPASS, or KYOTE.

Strategy 15: ACT Standards Tables—Explanation

In order for students to take ownership of their personal benchmarking process, the ACT Standards Tables were important tools. There were four tables that outline a continuum of skills necessary for success on the ACT in English, math, reading, and science. These four tables clearly showed the sets of skills necessary for a student to score within a certain ACT range (that is, 13–15, 16–19, 20–23, etc.) in each tested area.

Because the college-ready benchmarks are an 18 in English, a 19 in math, and a 20 in reading, students focused on that band of skill development that should help them score in the "20–23" range. Students received these sheets and kept them in their student data notebooks (specific content sheets in each ELA or math notebook). As students developed their skills, they monitored their progress toward successfully entering the "20–23" band. Once they were there and their confidence level regarding those skills was high, they were ready to attempt the COMPASS or KYOTE assessments in that content area (or take the ACT when given on a regular Saturday national test date).

An ACT document is available at http://www.act.org/standard/instruct/pdf/CollegeReadinessStandardsTables.pdf.

Strategy 16: Extra Opportunities to Meet Benchmarks—Explanation

The simplest way for a student to meet the ACT benchmarks required to be college ready was to successfully surpass them during a regularly scheduled national administration of the exam—usually proctored on a Saturday up to six times per year at an approved ACT test site. Students become college ready when they met the benchmark minimums *once*. They did not have to meet all three of the benchmarks in one sitting during one test administration to be college ready. They just needed to meet each benchmark once in each area before graduation to be fully college ready.

In addition, the students could take the COMPASS test at the school in each unmet benchmark area twice per year. They could also take the KYOTE assessment periodically after intervention periods to meet these benchmarks. In the case study school, senior students were more successful at meeting the benchmarks with the COMPASS than the KYOTE (fifty-seven benchmarks were met by seniors using the COMPASS compared to one student passing the KYOTE).

One *extra* benchmarking opportunity that case study school students took advantage of was the opportunity to COMPASS test on campus while taking a college visit. This additional COMPASS test did not count against the limit of two per student per year at the high school. Instead, a student told the university that he or she wanted to take a placement test to determine which courses he or she should enroll in during his or her freshman year of college. The college gladly administered the test because of the potential for that student to enroll in university classes the next semester. When the student finished, the campus testing administrator gave him or her a printout detailing his or her performance and whether or not he or she passed successfully.

Students brought these printed score sheets back to the high school and turned them in to the school counselor. If they successfully met the benchmark, they were one-third closer to their college readiness goals before graduation.

6

Establishing a MONITORING Method among Your Teachers

Purpose

> We humans are such creatures of habit, we'll keep doing
> something even though it's not working well—if it can be
> crossed off the list and somehow assumed valuable.

Stephen Wilson was a good principal. He had come up through
the ranks, loved working with kids and developing his staff,
and loved his hometown. To have the opportunity to lead the
local high school was a dream come true, and he was focused on
doing everything he could to grow a great school for the community. But on the phone this morning with his superintendent,
he realized there was much urgent work to be done. Junior and
senior class test results had fallen yet again, dropouts were up,
and successful transition to postsecondary was in the bottom
third of the state.

"I'm not scolding you, Stephen. When I'm in that building, I
feel the excitement, and the culture is steadily improving. Parents are telling me all the time how they can see the difference
you are making. I am just perplexed that this key bit of data on
your upperclassmen is so dismal. What is your theory on this
lack of some type of gains after all the extra resources we are
pumping into that school? Freshmen and sophomores are looking very strong. What's the common denominator here?"

Stephen blurted out before he meant to what he had realized
needed to be addressed. "PLCs."

"What?"

"Our PLCs, sir. We have had significant training in this area. Our teachers are all working in professional learning communities by meeting regularly to look at student data, and then providing interventions as needed—not just after the end of a six-week grading period. My underclassmen staff get it, and those PLCs are working well. But my teachers who work predominantly with our juniors and seniors—they struggle with this philosophy. They've never had to do it before, most are veteran teachers, and frankly, they've allowed their PLCs to become dysfunctional."

"Can you coach them along? Can you fix this?"

"I'll do my best, sir."

Stephen hung up the phone and sighed in frustration. He had known this was a problem but had been putting off addressing it. Now, he realized it was way past time. He opened his door and went to the outer office, adding to the afternoon announcements that he would meet with the PLC team leads the following day after school.

The next morning, Stephen made sure to not have anything scheduled after school that would rush this meeting. "I called you all to meet with me today because I need to sit in on your upcoming PLC sessions before fall break, and I wanted to get everyone on my calendar."

"Why, Mr. Johnson? We've had the training, and frankly, we've complied despite our misgivings." Shirley McCann had taught at this school for twenty-five years and was the self-appointed voice for the staff who worked with graduating seniors.

Stephen was incensed by the obvious defensive push-back, but kept his cool. "Shirley, I've made copies for all of you of the most recent data reports the district office has run for us. We're moving our younger kids along nicely, but our older students— especially our seniors—wow, the results are still not showing any gains. And an alarming number are dropping out of school."

"And that would be their prerogative at their age, right? Isn't that what the law says?" Shirley was tired of the innuendos that she was not a good teacher. And this young man half her age was not going to shove this nonsense down her throat anymore.

Stephen seized the opportunity. Shirley had opened the door for a real, transparent conversation. As the rest of the group looked at him, wondering how Shirley could resist so assertively, he calmly said, "And this is why we need to start over with our PLC process. So let's discuss around the table, one by one and with mutual respect for each other, where we truly are and why. Then we'll develop a plan that will get us where we need to be."

Shirley turned red and sat down. She knew her bluff had been called. On this day, her time was up. She did not say a word as the rest of her colleagues began seriously addressing the reality of why their collaborative teams were not working. Stephen took notes for several minutes. When everyone had taken their turn to share from their own perspective, he simply asked, "So what do we need to do differently so we are intervening for these kids and getting them to the finish line?" The conversation turned from frustration and helplessness to problem solving. One by one, the ideas flowed.

"We're not looking at the data the right way. We see it as our enemy."

"Our meetings are not organized. We do a lot of talking, but we don't have a protocol in place. You know, when to begin and how to allow everyone plenty of time to talk and reflect on individual students and their issues."

"Who takes notes, how to assign and take ownership on follow-up, when to end."

"And pray tell, why do we keep talking about home visits but they never happen?"

"And only talking about helping the counseling department with taking the seniors to visit campuses and other schools they might be interested in?"

"I had two seniors last year who were interested in the Army Reserves. I assumed they had joined up, but found out over the summer they were just hanging out downtown. I feel bad that I didn't help them to explore the military. Would have been so good for them at this stage of their lives."

"I had several girls who all claimed they were interested in nursing school. I did the same thing—assumed and did not provide the support I could have. Should have met with their parents and made sure they knew what the process was for applying to nursing school and how important their kids' assessment scores, especially in the sciences, would be. "

Stephen smiled. "Shirley, I do believe they get it. Thank you for diving deeper so we would lay all of this out on the table."

Questions for Reflection/Discussion:

1. Do your school's PLCs (or faculty teams that assess student work) have an effective protocol in place that is growth mindset driven?
2. Are these teams compliance oriented or results oriented?
3. Are these teams focused on students as individuals with real lives or assessment results only? Do they develop and monitor intervention plans for students?

Specific Strategies to Establish a MONITORING Method in Teachers

Strategy 17: Understanding Where My Students Are—Explanation

Student Ownership has focused primarily on ways to help the students take responsibility for their learning. Students examined their own data to find their growth areas. Students practiced the types of questions that they usually failed until they succeeded. Many strategies have been presented in this work that helped the students monitor and reflect on their learning. However, what should the teachers be doing to help this student ownership process be successful? How should teachers be reflecting?

Within professional learning community groups, teachers should continuously examine their practices and their students' results in order to promote lasting improvements in classroom instruction. Each classroom set of students is unique in their experiences, abilities, and skill levels. Why should we assume that a single teaching style (that often has not been changed very much in a decade or more) will be effective with all learners? Does that really make sense?

In the case study school, content-area professional learning community groups continuously examined their students' formative, interim, and summative assessment performance data and asked themselves four critical questions posed by DuFour, Dufour, Eaker, and Many (2006) in *Learning by Doing* (p. 91):

- What do we want our students to learn? (Curriculum/ Instruction)
- How will we know if each student learned it? (Assessment)
- How do we respond when some students do not learn it? (Reteaching/Intervention)
- How do we respond when students have learned it? (Enrichment/Extension)

It is only through this examination of practice and results that teachers could truly create responsive classrooms that met the needs of their current group of students. This ownership initiative required that students become reflective learners. The adults that facilitate this learning needed to become reflective teachers as well in order to be truly effective with each unique group of learners.

Strategy 18: Demystifying Testing—Explanation

Another important aspect of student ownership of their learning was to help students come to the understanding that testing success could be *helpful* to them. Testing success could lead to scholarships. Testing success could lead to credit for classes without actually taking them in college. Testing success could lead to higher pay because of a stronger transcript and more impressive resume. Testing success (in Kentucky) led to more state scholarship money upon graduation and enrollment in college.

For too long, teachers in some schools have used tests as negative, threatening events designed to "keep students in line" and "show them what they still have to learn." These tests (and the grades that result) have been used punitively for poor performance. Success research indicates that students are far more likely to respond with increased effort if they experience success instead of failure. Tests should be viewed by students as opportunities to show their knowledge. If students are fully prepared for the assessment (because they have mastered the standards and *know* that they are prepared fully), then the assessment should not be a dreaded event.

In the case study school, several steps were important in demystifying testing:

1. Students should understand the *value* of the test. Why does this test matter? How will it help me? Does it help me meet a benchmark? How?
2. Students should understand the *content* of the test. If the test matches the mastered standards and the questions are fair and open, then the student who has content knowledge should have assessment success.
3. Students should understand the *format* of the test. Are the selective response questions clear? Can I eliminate responses before answering to narrow down my choices? Are the extended written response questions clearly related to knowing or applying content I have learned? Are rubrics provided so that I understand the assessment expectations?

Tests should not create anxiety in fully prepared students. In the case study school's vocational courses (which produced the second-highest percentage of career-ready students in the state among 231 high schools), seniors in the automotive repair course took an industry certification test near the end of the year. The national pass rate for this exam is approximately 50 percent. The case study school students passed this test at a 98 percent rate. Why was this the case? What was this automotive repair teacher doing differently?

In the case study school automotive classes, students were taught the basics of automotive repair, then issued repair orders as if they worked in a functioning garage. Under the watchful eye of the instructor, they researched and then began work on fixing the problem in an actual automobile. The instructor only worked to facilitate their work. He let them make mistakes. When they called him in to consult, he did not give them the answers. He only asked probing questions to lead them to discovering the answers themselves.

After a year of this work, plus practice assessments that mirror the automotive repair industry certificate exam, the students were anxious to take and pass the exam. This test mattered to them because it was a validation of their hard work throughout the year and a payoff for their efforts. The students understood the value, the content, and the format of the test. There was very little mystery as to whether or not they would pass.

7

Establishing an INTERVENTION System among Your Students

Cruisin'

The road to success and fulfillment is narrow and steep.
Shortcuts along the way rarely lead to the "promised land."

James slept in and finally showed up at school during third period. He had led his basketball team in scoring the night before—a road game. The team bus had arrived back in town after 11 p.m.

"Missed you in ACT prep again, James. Third time this term."

"No sweat, Ms. Robinson. I got it all under control." James smiled and winked, as if to say, "I've got a plan."

Ms. Robinson was faculty advisor to the senior class and held weekly tutoring sessions for athletes. She had seen too many kids with promising futures somehow not understand how important these next few months would be. She knew James needed to get his ACT up several points, and time was running out.

But James was preoccupied. By Christmas break, he was leading the region in scoring, and some sports reporters were touting him as a shoo-in for all-state. His AAU coach kept him updated daily on what colleges were scouting his games. He just didn't have time for his studies, much less extra practice for some kind of national exam. When his midyear grades revealed he barely passed fall term, his high school coach made an appointment with Ms. Robinson.

"Coach, I know, I know. He's struggling and doesn't even realize what this means. He has distractions in his life that he thinks are harmless, but in the meantime he's only a few months away from graduating. What can we do to get him focused on his GPA and his ACT?"

"Maybe I'll invite his Uncle Bob to come in for a visit. I coached him years ago, and the sky was the limit with what he could have done in college and in life. He had it all . . . size, quickness, great shot, practiced and played hard every day, decent grades. He was offered an athletic scholarship and was on his way. But he dropped out of college his first semester and never returned."

James was dunking in warmups when he looked up and saw his uncle. He was in shock. Uncle Bob had not even come to one game this year. After practice, James went over and gave one of his life heroes a hug. "What brings you to town, ol' man?"

"Wow, my nephew sure is all grown up. Look at you. I hear you're burning the nets up this year, dude."

"Doin' alright, I guess." James tried to hide a sheepish grin.

"So I guess you're goin' to play college ball. How cool is that?"

"Yeah, that's the plan."

"What school?"

"Aww, I don't know yet. Several have sent letters. My AAU coach is working on some things."

"I guess you know a lot of that depends on your grades and your ACT, right?"

"Well, I figure if they want me to help them win a championship, they'll find a way to get me in."

"James, it doesn't work that way, son. As good as you are at playing basketball, there aren't any schools worth their salt who will offer you a scholarship unless you can meet their entrance requirements."

"Oh, Uncle Bob, come on. You know they bend the rules all the time. You were on scholarship. But you couldn't play with the big boys."

"Is that what you think happened to me? Well, James, sit down here for a minute. Let me tell you the truth. You see, I made better grades than you. And I was not in any danger of missing out on my one big chance due to my application being weak. I had made it, son. I had made the big time. All I had to do was work hard—one day at a time, one game at a time. But you see, I didn't have what it takes. I could not see four years down the road and what a college degree would mean for me and a future with a good job, nice income, using my talents to live a good life."

"Why did you quit, Uncle Bob?"

"My coach that freshman year was teaching all of us about being a team, not individual stars. I wasn't getting much playing time, so one day I just took a bus home. Thought I would teach him a lesson . . . worst decision of my life, James. I regret it every day."

James looked down at the floor—the floor he had grown up on playing ball. He could not imagine life without basketball. He put his arm around his uncle and just held on to him for a while.

The winter flew by. James led his team to the state playoffs and set the single-season scoring record for his school. After his last game, he realized he wanted so, so much to get serious about his studies and not let his dreams slip away. He hit the books, finally started attending Ms. Robinson's tutoring sessions, and waited and waited for an offer to come. But it never did. Several of his buddies were going to college. So were his girl cousins and friends from church. He couldn't believe it. What had he done wrong?

James stopped by Ms. Robinson's office at midsummer, and sure enough, she was there—tirelessly working on details for the junior class, now her new seniors.

"James, good to see you, young man."

"Hello, Ms. Robinson. I was just wondering. What do you think I should do now?"

"Well, there is a little college I have been in contact with that tells me if you will go to our local community college this fall and take remedial courses, they'd like for you and Coach to come visit them next spring. They do like the way you play ball."

"Hmm, I guess I could think about it."

"Have you thought about what you might want to major in, James? You know, what would you want to do as a career?"

"I'm going to play basketball ma'am. That's all I know to do."

James blew out his knee later that summer playing a pickup game at the Y. He never went to college. Often, down through the years, he thought about his Uncle Bob. And he thought a lot about way back there in seventh grade, when his studies started slipping because he spent all of his time playing basketball. And he thought about Ms. Robinson and that ACT test. And he finally understood.

Questions for Reflection/Discussion:

1. Does your school district have a systemic plan for every high school student to be prepared for college and other postsecondary entrance exams?
2. What is your community's philosophy in regard to the balance between academics and sports programs?
3. Do you know a high school student who is putting off or falling behind in the preparation needed for being ready for college? What intervention is needed?

Specific Strategies to Establish INTERVENTION in Students

Strategy 19: Transition Course Interventions—Explanation

In the explanation of students' assignment to transition courses, the *motivational* reasons why students were assigned were explained. In this description, the *intervention* processes are addressed.

All seniors in the case study school were enrolled in English IV (advanced seniors are enrolled in college-level ENG 101/102 for dual credit from the participating university). This senior-level English/language arts course was a graduation requirement for all seniors. If students have met the ACT benchmarks in reading (20) and English (18), then this course was all that is required.

However, if students had not met one of these benchmarks, then a second transitional ELA course was required to help them reach the ACT college-ready goals. Students were assigned to a transitional course within their seven-period day. This caused the loss of a free period when they would normally take one of their elective courses. It was hoped that this loss of elective was temporary and that the student could return to the elective once the benchmark was met.

Within the transition course, the focus was on diagnosis and treatment of the specific issues that prevented the student from meeting the ACT goal. Students took practice assessments (both pencil/paper and online) and used the results to determine their growth needs. Significant emphasis was placed on reflective use of the results by the students themselves in order for them to *own* this growth area and take responsibility for their own future academically. Yes, the ability to leave this transition course once the benchmark(s) was met is motivational, but the emphasis was on meeting the goal for future literacy and future life success, whether it be in postsecondary education or in the workforce.

In the case study school, a student had multiple opportunities to meet the benchmark *once practice assessment data proved the student was ready* to be successful.

- **ACT:** The senior could register and take the ACT exam during any of the six national test dates throughout the school year. The school served as a Saturday morning testing center, so transportation to a distant test site was not a barrier. Because we were a high-poverty school (nearly 80 percent of our students qualified for the federal free/reduced lunch program), ACT fee waivers were available for most students up to twice per year. This made the ~$40 cost of the assessment to students a nonissue as well. If a student met the benchmarks on this test, he or she was allowed to immediately transition from the course back to a desired elective.
- **COMPASS (at school):** If the student did not pass/take the ACT, the COMPASS test was an option. It is structured quite differently than the ACT exam. Whereas the

ACT is a timed paper-and-pencil test, the COMPASS is an untimed online test. Students are allowed unlimited time to read and be successful on the COMPASS exam. The school was allowed to administer the COMPASS twice per year to all students who had not yet met benchmarks. Usually, it was administered near midyear, then again at the end of the year. The midyear administration allowed for students who met the mark to make a schedule change and return to a desired elective at the semester break.

Students who were not successful on the ACT were often successful on the COMPASS due to the different format and lack of time limitations. It should be noted that student interviews suggested that because the format is somewhat different, the students felt far more confident to pass the COMPASS assessment the second time they attempted it—once they had a full understanding of the test format and structure.

- **COMPASS (on college campuses):** Another COMPASS opportunity that did not count against the limit of two assessments per student per school is the opportunity to take the same assessment on a college campus during a college visit. Colleges would gladly administer the COM-PASS assessment while a student was visiting on campus. This was viewed by the college as a potential step for that student to enroll and attend that institution. After the student completed the assessment, he or she received a printout of his or her scores that he or she brought to the school and placed on file with the transition teacher and school counselor. If the benchmark was met, the student could commence the schedule change process to exit the transition course.
- **KYOTE:** One additional benchmarking opportunity for students in the case study school's state was to pass the KYOTE (Kentucky Online Testing) assessment. This computer-driven assessment will also fulfill the bench-mark requirement. It is available at any point of the year. KYOTE regulations require that a twelve-week course of study be completed between administrations of the

assessment unless a student missed the passing mark by just a point or two. In that case, an immediate retest was permissible.

Of course, the specific tests, benchmarks, and processes used to indicate college readiness for a student vary state by state. Each school should examine its own state regulations to find every opportunity for a student to be successful.

Regardless of the process, it was very important to talk in terms of how students can meet their benchmarks (ownership language). The adults in the building were encouraged not to use language focused on themselves, such as "This will make me happy" or "I'll be so proud of you." Instead, the focus was placed on how these assessments will help the student be successful in the future (for example, additional scholarships, eliminate cost of remedial courses, more career choices).

Strategy 20: Intervention Software—Explanation

In order to meet the diverse needs of the transition course, a variety of differentiated teaching methods and supports were used. In some cases, educational software programs were useful to provide for the variety of needs within the transitional classroom. (While the case study school was not an affluent school with a large tax base, creative use of district and federal funding combined with grant funds allowed for this variety of software to be utilized.)

- Software used: ThinkLink Assessment Software
  http://www.discoveryeducation.com/administrators/assessment/
  Purpose: Used as a universal screener, this software assessment system provided information related to specific skill deficits that could be addressed using appropriate intervention strategies.
- Software used: TCA (Triumph College Admissions)
  http://www.tcaprep.com/sg/studyguide.php
  Purpose: Students took practice ACT exams and then worked on specific skill deficits indicated by results.

- Software used: ALEKS Math
  http://www.aleks.com/
  Purpose: Transitional math coursework used within senior math lab. Self-adjusted to the needs of the individual student based on progress through an online course. Program used many pre- and posttests to check for progress.
- Software used: WinLearn
  http://www.winlearning.com/
  Purpose: Self-guided course work for college and career readiness success. Students "leveled up" as they progressed through seven levels of learning in areas such as Reading for Information, Applied Math, and Locating Information (the three tested areas of the Work-Keys assessment). Additional academic and workplace principles modules were helpful with the attainment of career readiness.

Some of these online resources were funded by grant funds. Others were a part of the district Title I allocation. However, none of these was successful unless the students understood how the specific resources would benefit them as they move through the program. Because they understand that the program was designed to discover the specific skill deficits that they had to work on to pass benchmarks, and then a few initial students met the benchmark goals and transition out of the course, the other students' desire to work through and practice specific skills increased because they saw the positive impact of this intervention work.

Strategy 21: Extended Learning Opportunities (Summer)—Explanation

Additional intervention was available in the case study school to remediate/accelerate students for the next school year. Traditionally, students lose academic momentum in the summer and the ensuing school year must begin with a period of remediating old content before exploring new learning. However, this continuum of programs was designed to sustain spring academic momentum through the summer and into the next school year.

An initiative to help remedy loss of momentum with many of the case study school's struggling students was the use of summer learning opportunities (see table 7.1). Students were encouraged to enroll in a variety of remedial or accelerated summer courses in order to help them be successful the next year.

The key here was that the students themselves had to understand why this time is valuable to them so they would attend and participate. The initial invitations were verbal and targeted to specific students that would benefit from these programs. The case study school convinced the students that if they chose to commit to any of these programs, they would greatly benefit from them over their high school career. An example of ownership language used to invite and encourage participation by students is noted here.

Summer Learning Opportunities:

Program: **Second Chance**
Description: For students just below the failing grade for the year—one week of remediation to meet passing grade requirements.
Invitation Language: *"You're so close. If you just finish these assignments you will not be required to take the entire course over again! You will be able to take that elective you want instead of repeating that course!"*

Program: **Credit Recovery**
Description: For students who failed an entire course and were in danger of not graduating with their peer group. Delivered as coursework via Edgenuity or Novel Star software.
Invitation Language: *"You learned a lot of content in that course, but you did not pass the tests or the projects. Let's give you the opportunity to pass a different format of that course so that you can still graduate with your friends."*

Program: **Benchmark Bootcamp**
Description: For graduates who still needed to meet benchmarks before enrolling in college in the fall. Diagnosis/

interventions ("bootcamp") provided through the local Adult Education Center.

Invitation Language: *"Let's save you some money on college courses. If you'll spend some time in the Adult Ed Center and then take another COMPASS test, you'll be able to start your college career on classes that count toward your major and skip the remedial course (time and expense)."*

Program: EarlyStart (for incoming ninth-grade students)

Description: For exiting eighth-grade students where test data indicated a possible struggle with high school academics. Summer enrollment in a half-credit Workplace Principles course. Students meet and work with high school staff, transition to a new building, and become comfortable with their new setting before fall classes begin in a success-driven program. If future academic problems developed, these students already had a half-credit head start on graduation and did not fall out of their peer group.

Invitation Language: *"You were chosen for this course so that you can get a head start on high school. You'll know where everything is, meet all of your teachers, and get a half-credit for doing it!"*

As you can see, great care was taken to convince students that these extended learning opportunities benefited them and that they were making a wise decision by choosing to participate. This was an important piece of helping these struggling students take ownership of their learning!

Table 7.1.   Summer Menu of Continuous Progress

Sample County High School Summer Learning Opportunities

(designed to remediate or extend the learning to increase success)

Program	Description	Dates
Second Chance	Additional instruction at LCHS for students who ended the year with 50 to 64 percent in a class—fifteen hours additional instruction/remediation and the possibility of earning the credit instead of failing the course.	May 20, 21, 22 (fifteen hours) 8:30–3:00 M, T 8:30–11:30 W
Credit Recovery	Internet coursework to help students make up a credit that they have failed. Students use Novel Star software to learn content and pass assessments. Must pass online assessments to receive credit for the course. Facilitated at the Area Technology Center.	May 27–June 14 8:30–11:30 daily
Benchmark Bootcamp	For recently graduated seniors— additional instruction through the Lee Adult Education Center to help graduates meet college benchmarks before June 30. For graduates who still need to meet one or two ACT college benchmarks before the fall.	Immediately after graduation. Meeting May 20 (C. Herald)
LCHS EarlyStart	For thirty eighth-grade students entering LCHS in the fall—nine-day course using LCHS and ATC staff in *Workplace Principles*—students earn half of an LCHS credit. Several benefits include: • Course will count in *all* career pathways, • Effective transition to LCHS from LCMS, • Familiarity with LCHS, ATC teachers, • Funded by Gear-UP, • Food and transportation provided.	May 28–June 7 8:30–3:00 daily

8

Establishing an INTERVENTION System among Your Teachers
Safety Net

One or two working on a project—transformation begins. A team focused on the same work—lives are changed.

Anthony threw his book bag on his bed in disgust. He had failed another class and hated school so much he was having anxiety attacks in the mornings. It was near the end of junior year, and his grade point average was now so low he might not be eligible for soccer his senior year. He would have to take summer school as well to even be classified as a senior. He opened his desk drawer and picked up the business card of a counselor in town his assistant principal had said was really good. He couldn't handle another year of school without some type of relief.

"So talk to me about these anxiety attacks. How long have you been having them?"

Anthony felt better just knowing he had finally had the courage to seek professional help. Mr. Jacobson was not a psychologist, but he was working on his doctorate. And he had a genuine style of conversation that was reassuring and nonjudgmental.

"They started about a year ago. I have really struggled in high school with my studies. Got behind my freshman year in Algebra I and Spanish, and it all went downhill from there. School used to be enjoyable, or at least manageable. And when it wasn't, my soccer got me through the rough times. I've never been an honor roll student, but I could hold my own—until these last couple of years. Now, I hate it. Literally, I've thrown up a couple of times in the shower before coming to school."

"Well, I can put you on some mild medicine for a few months that will help you with the anxiety. But I want you to let me try something first, Anthony. Will you meet with me after school one day soon, along with your principal and senior counselor?"

"Sure, whatever you think will help."

A week later Anthony anxiously sat in the main office at school and smiled when he saw Mr. Jacobson parking in the visitors' space out front.

"Principal Hawkins, I have a huge favor to ask. I am working on my doctorate, and my dissertation is on school intervention programs. If I were to be, say, in Anthony's shoes—going into my senior year after summer school—what would you recommend for me as I came back this fall?"

Without hesitation, Mr. Hawkins, who had been at the helm at this school for twelve years, said, "Get heavily involved with our faculty/student mentoring program. We're just beginning year two, and we've already seen tremendous results. For the first time, I'm embarrassed to say, we are providing the array of types of support our seniors need in their last year with us."

"But it's only for seniors?"

"No, not anymore. Last year, we piloted it with our seniors. Guess what? Less attrition. Record number of graduates going to postsecondary. Record number of scholarships."

"Would you let me study this initiative this coming year— for my research? Allow me to come to school from time to time, observe this model in action, interview students, interview teachers, interview parents?"

"Yes, sir, I would be glad to help make that happen. And better yet, I'd love to put you on our development team for working out the kinks in the program as we expand in year two. Could you work with Mrs. Hutchinson here, our senior class counselor, in refining our model this summer?"

"How about if Anthony joins us as your student representative?"

"Okay. I'll allow that. And I'll add a couple of classroom teachers, another student, and the other three counselors as well."

And so Anthony's transformation began that day. As the summer unfolded, he couldn't believe he was on this influential team that was creating such a major support system for his classmates. And when fall term rolled around, he didn't have anxiety issues the first week like he had assumed he would. Instead, he was focused on the faculty/student mentoring program he had helped develop. The curriculum was amazing, and oh how he wished he could go back and be in ninth grade again. What a difference it would have made.

Beginning the first week of the semester, every student in the school met with their faculty mentor twice a month during a fifty-minute block that rotated through the various periods of the day. Each mentor only worked with students they had a trusting connection with, either through earlier classes, a club, coaching, community activities, or in another relationship capacity. "Life skills" issues were discussed, how to fill out applications, test taking strategies, healthy boundaries, time management, goal setting, and leadership training. And guest speakers often joined this protected time with wonderful tips and suggestions about real life.

Ironically, as Anthony had not a clue what he was going to do after high school, it was in one of these mentoring sessions in November that he listened intently to the recruiter who explained what serving in the armed forces meant—with the advanced training, travel, and other benefits. Anthony couldn't believe it. So he could sign up, fulfill his contract, and this would make him eligible for going back to school to train in whatever vocation he wanted to make as his career? He had found his answer. He had never felt so called before to serve and make a difference. This was his niche. Finally, he knew what he wanted to do next in his life.

And Anthony was not alone. His senior class again set new records for graduates, those going on to specialized training after high school, and scholarships. Anthony's school was no longer a prison for the kids who could not keep up the rigorous pace or who had just stopped trying. Now, it was a bridge to the exciting world they had dreamed of way back when they were children in elementary school. Yes, it was changed—much less a school with too few winners and too many losers. Now it was an innovative community of hope, where lives were changed—every day.

Questions for Reflection/Discussion:

1. Does your high school's faculty/student mentoring program provide a planned curriculum that emphasizes life skills and systemic individualized mentoring for all students?
2. If not, what is the alternative model that provides systemic individualized mentoring for all students?
3. Is every student in your high school working on a personalized growth plan that details step by step his or her roadmap through high school and into postsecondary?

Specific Strategies to Establish INTERVENTIONS for Teachers

Strategy 22: Using the "Persistence to Graduation" Report for At-Risk Students—Explanation

One of the tools that the case study school used to identify at-risk students for mentoring and intervention was the Infinite Campus student information system report titled "Persistence to Graduation." This early dropout warning report could be generated at any time during the school year. The program pulls relevant student data from the database and generates a list of students most likely to drop out of school based on historical data trends.

When the "Persistence to Graduation" report was run, each student in the school was ranked on a 0 to 13 scale based on the likelihood that the student would not finish high school.

The criteria used within the program to rank the potential drop-out students are:

- Gender
- Absences
- Courses completed
- Courses failed
- Behavioral referrals
- Suspensions
- Current grades

Using a predetermined formula, students were rated from 0 (small chance of dropping out) to 13 (greatest possibility of dropping out).

In the case study school, this report was produced every four weeks. Current grade sheets were printed for the students at the top of the report and distributed to 1) the principal, 2) counselor, and 3) teacher(s) who had established authentic mentoring relationships with these students as described earlier. These individuals began an intensive mentoring session with their student mentee(s) and searched for the root causes and solutions to help the student(s) be successful.

Strategy 23: RtI for College/Career Readiness—Explanation

For the seniors involved in this case study, the desired outcome was attainment of the college benchmarks (ACT English 18, Math 19, and Reading 20). The school's Response to Intervention Plan (RtI) for seniors was focused on attainment of these goals because meeting these benchmarks indicated college readiness, as well as the academic component of career readiness. Student ownership of the learning in these classes was quite high because of the students' desire to move from these transition/RtI Tier II classes back to a desired elective course.

Case Study School: Senior RtI Plan for English/Language Arts

Tiers of Intervention: College and Career Readiness for Seniors (English/Reading)

Table 8.1.

Tier	Description of Tier	Lee County CCR Implementation
Tier I	Foundational: Standards-Driven Instruction for All Students (Benchmark)	• All senior students receive standards-based instruction within their English IV or dual-credit English 101/102 senior core English courses. • All seniors enroll in one of these two course options regardless of whether they have met the English and reading ACT benchmarks or not.
Tier II	Supplemental: Interventions for Some At-Risk Students (Strategic)	• Seniors who have not met the English and/or reading benchmarks are enrolled in a second senior ELA course (a transitional course called Reading for College Success). • This course diagnoses and remediates specific issues (in large groups, small groups, or individually). • Diagnostic and reteaching software TCA and WinLearn are used in addition to classroom tiered instruction. • Once the benchmark is met by either ACT, COMPASS, or KYOTE assessment success, the student transfers back to Tier I and out of the transition course. This allows the student to return to a desired elective.
Tier III	Supplemental: Interventions for High-Risk Students (Intensive)	• Students received intensive one-on-one instruction from a reading specialist during their transition course period. Specific diagnostic records were kept to ensure that the student was making sufficient progress.

Case Study School: Senior RtI Plan for Math

Tiers of Intervention: College and Career Readiness for Seniors (Math)

Table 8.2.

Tier	Description of Tier	Lee County CCR Implementation
Tier I	Foundational: Standards-Driven Instruction for All Students (Benchmark)	• All senior students receive standards-based math instruction within their math courses. All seniors have two math classes. Seniors that have met benchmarks have Pre-Calculus, Calculus, or dual-credit College Algebra MAT 107.
Tier II	Supplemental: Interventions for Some At-Risk Students (Strategic)	• All seniors who have not met benchmarks have Algebra III and/or Math for Business and Industry. Both of these courses have interventions embedded. • This course diagnoses and remediates specific issues (in large groups, small groups, or individually). • Diagnostic and reteaching software Aleks, TCA, and WinLearn are used in addition to classroom tiered instruction. • Students meet the benchmark on the ACT assessment, COMPASS, or KYOTE exams.
Tier III	Supplemental: Interventions for High-Risk Students (Intensive)	• Students received intensive one-on-one instruction from a math teacher during their transition course period. Specific diagnostic records were kept to ensure that the student was making sufficient progress.

9

Establishing a CELEBRATION System among Your Students

Honoring the Work (and Those Who Do It)

> Joy at work is not an illusion. Some organizations do indeed create such a mood of celebration of the people who are the reason for the successes. And thus, those in the trenches don't dread coming to work. They thirst for it.

Ted threw on his clothes and was off to school. His senior class was having a recognition breakfast that would take up most of the morning. The combined results of this group of students had set new records at the school. Dignitaries from the community, faculty, and staff—everyone was going to be involved in the celebration. And Ted would be called up front at some point to be congratulated for his part in the overall success. He had worked hard to improve his ACT and vocational competency scores and the state exams. And he had exceeded even his own expectations—with the tireless help of his teachers and his peer tutor.

This culture of care and focus on the students had not always been the ethos of Ted's high school. During his first three years, he had hated school. The daily routines were rigid and boring. The classwork was too programmed. Students produced out of fear or obligation instead of motivation. The environment was more like a prison than a twenty-first-century school.

But all of that changed at the beginning of Ted's senior year. A new principal and assistant principal had arrived last summer. Mr. Thomas had come from out of town after a stellar career leading schools to unparalleled success. And Mrs. Templeton had been promoted from within the ranks as a teacher at another school in the district to assistant principal. From the first day, it was a new beginning.

As he drove to school, Ted relived his exit interview with his senior counselor the day before. He had not been able to hide his excitement.

"The opening day assembly was about student successes, and Mr. Thomas had explained a huge graphic on a big screen that described in detail what his expectations were for this school year. He didn't miss anything. From academics, to the music and 'arts' programs, to increased participation in the clubs, to athletics—he challenged the student body as never before. I remember thinking to myself, 'I like this guy already.'"

"Ted, tell me more about this transformation of culture. Could you feel it in the classroom as well?" The counselor's questions were probing, and Ted enjoyed this opportunity to really share his experiences and feelings about the school. Mrs. Templeton had been the reason for these exit interviews, asking how the school could improve if students didn't weigh in with the realities—good and bad, and all in between.

"My classes were different this year. Teachers seemed happier and more creative. We were engaged in more projects instead of mainly textbooks. We read a lot, sure, but the goal seemed to be about how to use our abilities to innovate and develop solutions. Students loved it."

"Did your parents notice your change in attitude toward school?"

"Yes, definitely. I remember Dad asking at supper one evening about halfway through the fall semester why I was making such better grades."

"What did you tell him?"

"I explained that school was fun again, like way back in my early years."

"So it was easier?"

"Not easier—no. Actually, more challenging. But I was engaged. The work was relevant."

"You mentioned project-based learning. Give me another example."

"Technology. For some reason, more of my classes allowed us to utilize technology in some way—if not daily at least several times a week. Not just the teacher using technology. We were diving into it ourselves. So, so cool."

"Another example?"

"Senior English class was fun. I couldn't believe it. But we had a new teacher come in this year, and she was all about preparing us for college or whatever we chose to go into after high school. Man, it was so interesting. We learned how to write about life—in our journals. I had never really done it that way before. We learned how to do a term paper—step by step—3 × 5 cards and all. And we learned how to take notes. She would pretend to be a professor and just go off on these fast lectures. I now know how to simply capture the main ideas—and I have my own version of shorthand."

"And on Fridays, she often invited in adults from all walks of life who shared about how communication was such a key part of their job. One guy was an auto mechanic, and he reminded us that if he wasn't friendly with his customers and couldn't carry on an intelligent conversation with them, he'd lose their business. . . . An auto mechanic in senior English—I loved that class."

"Exams? Your class made huge assessment gains this year. How did that happen?"

"Simple. Mrs. Templeton worked with all our teachers, and us too, and showed us the road map for improving test scores. We had never really been put on a plan that detailed. And Mr. Thomas and Mrs. Templeton believed in us—every day. From morning announcements, to inspirational talks at pep rallies, to how they and the teachers treated us—all around the building. It mattered."

"Give me some more examples."

"Well, for one, Mr. Thomas was great at stopping by at lunch or even riding with us on field trips. He knew our names, and he was interested in our lives. And Mrs. Templeton started these small groups where she would meet with seniors and just chat with us about life. She was always stressing that we be prepared for what came after high school. Actually, it was her who motivated me to visit a couple of schools I'm thinking about next year."

"And what came of that?"

"You know, it helped me to realize I really do enjoy working with my hands—a lot. My dad owns his own heating and air conditioning company, and I've learned some things about that line of work. So I'm enrolling in the local technical college's HVAC program this fall. We'll see what happens."

"Anything else, Ted, you'd like to add?"

"Just that this year was about people. One morning Mr. Thomas mentioned in his announcements that one of our freshman girls had been accepted to an elite ballet school she will be attending this coming summer. Another time he congratulated one of our sophomore guys for winning a bass fishing tournament. And he would praise staff too—sometimes even about their life accomplishments outside of school. He would do things the like that all the time, reminding all of us of our unique gifts and abilities—and that he cared."

"And it sounds like his attitude rubbed off on others."

"Oh yes. I noticed it all the time. The front office lady was friendlier. The cafeteria staff loosened up and smiled more when we went through the line. Even the custodians seemed to enjoy their work more."

"Ted, this 'joy at work,' which seems to be what you are describing, what's the key ingredient?"

"Celebrating the people and their work. Turning them loose to create, explore, learn by trial and error."

"Sounds like this culture of celebration in your senior year has been a blessing for you, Ted."

"Has changed my entire attitude about learning and about what I am capable of. And also how to treat other people. . . . It's changed my life."

Questions for Reflection/Discussion:

1. How does your school culture compare to the one described here?
2. What changes has your principal and staff implemented in your building to be considered a model twenty-first-century school?
3. What kinds of celebrations does your school enjoy throughout the year? How often do these take place? What percentage of students and staff are recognized? (Are these mainly for athletics, or do they encompass the entire school community and its work?)

Specific Strategies to Establish CELEBRATIONS for Students

Strategy 24: Student Results Celebration—Explanation

The PowerPoint referenced in this chapter marked an important milestone in the student ownership process each year. It served to "pass the baton" from the graduated and departed seniors to the next year's group of current (and future) twelfth graders.

Many of the accountability measures for our students were administered at the very end of the school year—right up and through the season of final examinations. Sharing this data with the student body was not possible until early fall when these scores are returned to the school as a part of our state accountability measures. In order to communicate with the students a report focused on how the school (and they as individuals) performed, the data were communicated with the entire student body in a celebration assembly. Upbeat music, bright lights, and smiles greeted the students as they filed into the auditorium. This was a celebration of their hard work.

The sixteen-slide PowerPoint presented here was a sample of what this type of assembly might look like in a school. It can be used as a template with local data for any school. It was intentionally crafted (along with the presentation by a school administrator) to communicate the following concepts:

1. Testing matters, and it matters to students individually.
2. People examine how students perform.
3. Test scores follow you throughout your career.
4. College expenses can be reduced if you meet benchmarks and attain better scholarships.
5. The only people who can change this data are the students.

In the case study school state, three important measures of effectiveness were: 1) percentile rank among all schools; 2) number of students that were college and/or career ready; and 3) graduation rate. Each of these measures was detailed in this report. Celebrations of success were loud and sustained. Improvement needs were also intensely communicated as the student's "next steps" in meeting a vision for continuous improvement.

The timing of this celebration was also painstakingly planned for maximum impact on multiple student groups.

1. This celebration was held the day before approximately one-fourth of the student body took a regular October Saturday administration of the ACT. The importance of doing well on this test was significantly communicated in this assembly.

2. This celebration was held on a Friday. On the following Monday, nonbenchmarked seniors were taking the Armed Services Vocational Aptitude Battery exam that can help meet the academic requirements of career ready. The types of questions, content areas assessed, and time of each section were communicated with all of these students so that the test format and expectations would be familiar the following school day. This serves to help the students understand what to do and, more importantly, why they need to be successful with the exam to help themselves.

3. The hour before this assembly, the principal took eighteen of his most challenging male students and had a one-hour seminar with them—communicating expectations for a change in academic behavior. He made these eighteen students sit with him during the assembly, then took them back to a conference room and had them reflect on what they had heard.

   The end result of this reflection and sharing was an increased focus for these sophomore boys on why they should take ownership of their learning. It was a successful intervention wrapped around a successful celebration assembly. Note: The principal continued to meet with these eighteen boys for lunch throughout the school year—working on study habits and success strategies. At the end of the year, the principal served as their test proctor. He invested in them, and a number of them made substantial gains on their assessments.

Each school will celebrate successes differently. Celebration in the case study school occurred in a variety of ways, including this assembly.

The PowerPoint template is included.

**Lee County
High School**

2012-2013 Student Results
Report

Three Measures of Success

o Percentile Ranking in KY
o College and Career Readiness
o Graduation Rate

o How did we do on these three measures?

Our Comparison Group

LCHS vs. 15 Surrounding School Systems

Measure #1: KY Academic Ranking

ο *Measured by: End-Of-Course Assessments, PLAN, ACT and 10th/11th Grade On-Demand Writing*

ο *How does our performance this year compare with our group?*

Percentile Ranking (of 231 KY High Schools):

	Percentile 2011-2012	Percentile 2012-2013
1. Jackson Independent	93rd	98th
2. Montgomery County	58th	87th
3. Estill County	27th	84th
4. Wolfe County	66th	81st
5. Lee County	57th	80th
6. Clark County	32nd	78th
7. Madison County	57th	76th
8. Owsley County	23rd	75th
9. Berea Independent	58th	62nd
10. Jackson County	11th	58th
11. Perry County	5th	55th
12. Knott County	37th	52nd
13. Powell County	20th	48th
14. Breathitt County	6th	26th
15. Clay County	10th	23rd
15. Magoffin County	9th	23rd

GREAT GAINS, LCHS!

o How do we get better?

o *END OF COURSE ASSESSMENTS – Learn the content and try hard on every test!!!!*

Measure #2: College/Career Readiness

o *Measured by:*
  o *College: ACT Benchmarks (or COMPASS or KYOTE)*
  o *Career: Academic Performance AND Technical Certificate*

o *2010-2011: LCHS had a 29 CCR Score*

o *2011-2012: LCHS had a 62.5 CCR Score*

o *2012-13: LCHS had a 81.3 CCR Score*

o *We ranked 26th in the state of 231 Schools!*

o *How does that compare with our group?*

College/Career Readiness Comparison to Area

2011 – 2012 C/CR		2012 – 2013 C/CR	
1. Jackson Ind	65	1. Lee County	81
2. Lee County	63	2. Jackson Independent	70
3. Montgomery Co	57	3. Montgomery County	68
4. Wolfe Co	53	3. Wolfe County	68
4. Berea Ind	53	5. Estill County	66
6. Clark	52	6. Perry County	54
7. Madison	50	6. Powell County	54
8. Powell Co	47	8. Clark County	53
9. Knott Co	44	9. Breathitt County	52
10. Estill Co	43	10. Berea Independent	51
11. Clay Co	41	10. Jackson County	51
11. Owsley Co	41	12. Magoffin County	50
13. Jackson Co	39	13. Owsley County	49
14. Breathitt Co	38	13. Clay County	49
15. Magoffin Co	37	15. Madison County	47
16. Perry Co	28	16. Knott County	45

C/CR Status update (for 2013-14 Seniors):

o As of this point, This year's Seniors are meeting ACT Benchmarks at a faster pace than last year's seniors!

2012-13 Seniors on October 15, 2012	2013-14 Seniors on October 15, 2013
25.6%	**33.3%**
Met all 3 Benchmarks	Met all 3 Benchmarks

College Readiness

o How do we get better?

o ACT, COMPASS and KYOTE

    o Use ACT Prep, WinLearn and Transition Courses to improve!

    o Take multiple chances to be successful!!!

Career Readiness
(Currently #2 in the State)

o How do we get better?

o Two Parts:

Academic:	Technical:
Benchmarks	KOSSA
(ACT, COMPASS, KYOTE)	or
or	Industry Certifications
ASVAB (TUESDAY!)	(ASE, NCCER,
or	IC3, Nurse Aid)
WorkKeys	

College/Career Readiness
(Currently #26 in the State)

o We get 1 point for College Ready

o We get 1 point for Career Ready

o We get 1.5 points for BOTH

Measure #3: Graduation Rate

o *Measured by:* The percentage of your group that become high school graduates in FOUR years.

o How does our performance this year compare with our group?

Graduation Rate:

2010-11 Graduation Rate			2011-12 Graduation Rate	
1.	Wolfe Co.	91.5%	1. Montgomery County	97.0%
2.	Jackson Ind.	82.8%	2. Berea Independent	95.8%
3.	Berea Ind.	80.0%	3. Estill County	95.7%
4.	Owsley Co.	79.6%	4. Jackson Independent	95.2%
5.	Madison Co.	78.8%	5. Owsley County	94.7%
6.	Perry Co.	78.3%	6. Powell County	93.5%
7.	Powell Co.	78.0%	7. Magoffin County	92.4%
8.	Knott Co.	77.1%	8. Madison County	92.3%
9.	Montgomery Co.	76.2%	9. Wolfe County	92.2%
10.	Magoffin Co.	76.0%	10. Clark County	90.1%
11.	Jackson Co.	73.8%	**11. Lee County**	**89.2%**
12.	Clark Co.	73.2%	12. Knott County	87.9%
13.	Estill Co.	70.9%	13. Jackson County	87.0%
14.	Clay Co.	67.8%	14. Breathitt County	86.5%
15. Lee Co.		**67.1%**	15. Clay County	83.4%
16.	Breathitt Co.	63.3%	16. Perry County	81.7%

Graduation Rate

o How do we get better?

o Don't get behind – each core course failed requires a re-take or a credit recovery the next year – which pulls you out of an elective!

o Attendance: Employers look at your high school attendance to see if they want to hire you!

Fact: We are currently at the 80th percentile state-wide

Goal for 2013-14:
90th Percentile Statewide
Clawing to the Top!

Strategy 25: College and Career Readiness
Thermometer—Explanation

Without a doubt, the celebration visual in the case study school that made the most impact on encouraging students to meet ACT benchmarks and industry certifications was created on a single sheet of poster board with red and black markers. This visual helped to change the topic of conversation within the senior class to meeting college and career readiness goals.

The concept was simple: create a "thermometer" of success that students would color in red as they met their college or career readiness goals. The case study school graduated eighty-three seniors, therefore each senior was approximately 1.2 percent of the entire senior class. Individual accomplishment becomes much more important when just a few students can move your success or failure rates dramatically. Each student, therefore, was ultimately responsible for a significant, visible section of the thermometer. If the thermometer was to rise, it would be up to each individual.

As students met benchmarks and reached career readiness, they were brought to the school foyer to color in *their personal* 1.2 percent "stripe" on the thermometer. Their picture was taken and displayed on the school electronic billboard (that is, flat-screen TV in the school entrance hall). They were excited to reach this milestone and receive recognition.

Students also liked to look at how their class compares to past senior classes. A note was kept on the thermometer reporting how the current class was performing compared to previous graduating classes. For instance, one October found that the current group of seniors was 8 percent ahead of the benchmark pace that the previous year's senior class had met at this date in the calendar. The students were quite proud of this success and talked about how they could stay ahead of the pace.

This ownership translated into increased focus and effort both on the ACT and within the classroom. Interestingly, when a school official met with the junior class last spring five days before the statewide administration of the ACT, the student response was unexpected. As the official talked about scholarships and the need to avoid remedial freshman college courses, one student in the class raised a hand and asked the one real question all juniors wanted answered: "When do we get our CCR thermometer?"

The focus and effort this visual created was impactful and lasting. This is a fantastic return for the investment of one sheet of poster board and a couple of red and black poster markers.

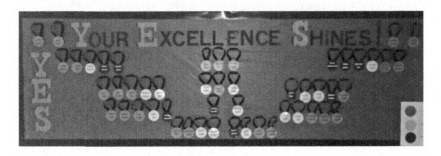

Strategy 26: Student Medals for Benchmarks—Explanation

Another visual celebration of student success was the placing of "medals" on a bulletin board in the hallway as each student met their benchmarks. The medals were on colored paper printed with the student's name: gold for all three benchmarks, silver for two, and bronze for meeting one of the benchmarks.

The board was initiated at the start of the senior year. Students who have met one, two, or all three benchmarks were allowed to personally post the appropriate medal on the board. As students met additional benchmarks throughout the year, they were allowed to replace the old medal with the appropriate new one as a celebration. If the change in medals was delayed for any reason, students who met their benchmarks often sought out the adult in charge so that the board could be updated to accurately reflect their performance.

This visual was created during the 2012 Olympics as a timely and fun celebration of success. However, the following year's seniors wanted it to be continued another year so that they could be recognized as well. This was a very inexpensive visual that every student walked past each day within the halls of the school and was prominently displayed near the front foyer entry door that students enter and exit. It served as a constant reminder of what we value academically and helped encourage students to reach for benchmark goals for themselves.

Strategy 27: Graduation Honor Cords—Explanation

During commencement at the case study school, graduates wore honor cords of different colors signifying outstanding achievement in specific areas (grade point average, student organization officers, and specific club activities). During this *Student Ownership* initiative, the school added a new honor cord color (silver) to recognize those students who were *both* college and career ready. This cord signified that the student had met all ACT benchmarks *and* had achieved a career-ready status through a technical certification.

The adults in the school made this honor important. It was a topic of discussion in all courses with a preponderance of seniors enrolled. For those students who had already achieved both college and career readiness, it was validation. For other students who were close, it became a goal that they feverishly wanted. School officials were forced to make extra trips to the out-of-town graduation supply house to purchase additional sets of silver cords because students continued taking benchmark assessments on local college campuses up to the day before graduation.

Why did a braided piece of silver string become so important to the seniors at the case study school?

Student interviews revealed that the cords became a symbol of senior year success. The school's change in culture led to a different definition of success by the end of the senior year. College and career readiness became important. Therefore, the symbol of success by that CCR definition became desired by students.

So passionate were the seniors to earn these cords that a group of students received permission to miss commencement practice two days before graduation in order to visit a local university for one more COMPASS test to meet their last unmet benchmark.

All members of the group were successful. All of them marched two days later with silver honor cords around their neck.

In all, 37 percent of the seniors in that graduating class met both college benchmarks and career readiness thresholds. This group of students in this state-designated PLA (persistently low achieving) school scored in the ninetieth percentile in college and career readiness and ranked 2 of 231 state high schools specifically in the career readiness measure.

10

Establishing a CELEBRATION System among Your Teachers

Culture

> People like to work. We're wired to create, to contribute
> with meaning that makes a difference. So when a workplace
> culture is unimaginative or employees are lined up at the
> door to leave, somewhere along the line, leadership has
> failed.

"Mrs. Adams, they're ready in the gym."

Jenny looked up from the computer to her faithful secretary. "Margie, you have been amazing these last few days, as always. With so much going on during the last week of the school year, I have been overwhelmed. So the staff is all out there too?"

"Everyone, Mrs. Adams. Students, staff, lots of parents, several from the board office. And oh, I almost forgot—the local television crew."

Jenny stopped at her office door and bowed her head. "Thank you." She offered praise as her mind raced back over these last three years.

She remembered her first day on the job. The janitors were arguing over who was supposed to wax the gym. She had one month before school started and a master schedule to update, three new teachers to hire, a month's worth of mail to sift through—some of it time sensitive from the central office. And it seemed that every staff person that came by to welcome her had a complaint to file of some kind. She had made sure she met everyone individually and taken plenty of time to ask them what was working and what was not working in this school. Whew! They were a broken lot.

She also remembered how her heart sank when she began looking over student achievement data. This was not only an underperforming high school, it was also at the bottom of the region. And a quick look at the school's policy manual indicated there was much work to be done in the area of protocol alone. There seemed to be few systems in place.

So Jenny had taken this giant of a mess and, one day at a time, modeled caring, dedicated, ethical leadership. In her first staff meeting, she celebrated what the school had done right. Teachers looked around at each other in shock. They had not been told they had a lot to be proud of in a long time.

In her first student assembly, she did the same—and had invited in a motivational speaker who was not only funny but also challenged the kids to make this the best year the school had ever experienced. They listened. They had thirsted for being asked to take it to a higher level.

From that first day, Jenny and a school management taskforce retooled the discipline protocol. She had appointed several students to this team as well. Within a week, teachers were coming to her office in shock, with smiles on their faces. They had not had such a peaceful, respectful, happy group of teens in this building in years.

And staff noticed how she never criticized anyone or talked sarcastically. Instead, she treated everyone she met—from parents with complaints to grumpy bus drivers and worn-out teachers—with respect and an attitude that said, "We can do this. We can find solutions. Together, if we believe in each other, support each other, and trust each other, nothing can stop us." And so the bickering and toxic habits steadily changed to a culture that was about other people. Caring for other people.

Jenny noticed early on that the teachers and their classroom assistants were conditioned to be told what to do—in every way. So she asked them to design an effective team structure that had them meeting monthly in their passion zones. If they were passionate about technology, she wanted that cluster of staff working together. If they loved designing curriculum, then that's where she wanted that set of teachers focused. And she turned them loose to explore the best professional development she could afford with her budget, based on their individual needs.

Often, she would send them to a nearby school to observe a model program in action. She empowered her staff to be better, and they responded in amazing ways. But she also put them in PLCs that met weekly, and she met with each of these professional learning communities on a rotation basis to help everyone focus on student achievement and effective interventions day by day.

In that first month of classes, Jenny visited every room. She had lunch in the cafeteria with students at their tables. She invited every parent—with letters mailed to home addresses—to come for an "evening with the principal." This question and answer session drew two hundred attendees. The usual parent night at this school had typically attracted fifty or less.

Jenny had noticed a one-dimensional philosophy toward students and their gifts and abilities. This school community lived for athletics and had indeed turned out some very successful sports teams over the years. But the academic team, the music program, the celebration of the "arts" in general, nonathletic extracurricular opportunities—they were not given much attention at all.

So she had begun the second six-week grading period with an assembly during which she rolled out a new definition of "menu of student services." When she introduced the dads who she had asked to organize a Saturday intramural program, applause erupted. And by year's end, the number of student clubs had doubled, and students joining the band tripled—because she believed in these programs and let everyone know they would be appreciated and honored from this point on.

And so it went—month by month, semester by semester. Jenny had modeled for the entire school community how to envision something special and then how to grow into greatness.

As she walked out onto the gym floor to find her seat behind the podium with the school district's superintendent, every person in the packed auditorium stood and gave Jenny an ovation that lasted what seemed like five minutes.

Superintendent Martin stood to speak. "Mrs. Adams, you have brought life, pride, and joy back to this school and the entire community. And yesterday afternoon, I received word from the state department that this school made more gains in student achievement than any other in this great commonwealth this past year. And you've hit the top-ten list overall. We just wanted to say thank you. You have shown all of us what it truly means to be a servant leader."

Jenny came forward to accept a plaque that had been given to the school by the local Rotary. It read: "Greatness is found in those who invest in the lives of others."

And she simply said: "The greatness is all of you. I knew you could do it. And you have. I am the one who is blessed—in countless ways every day."

Questions for Reflection/Discussion:

1. How does your school community celebrate the successes of students and faculty?
2. What training and support does your school leadership and staff need in transitioning to a comprehensive student success model?
3. What needs to take place for your school to grow away from toxic culture issues?

Specific Strategies to Establish CELEBRATIONS for Teachers

Strategy 28: Celebrations with Teachers (Small Successes)—Explanation

As previously stated, the teachers in the case study school were demoralized when the institution was designated by the state Department of Education as a PLA (persistently low achieving) school based on school accountability measures. In order to change to a student-centered success culture, the staff needed to own the student successes as well.

No public school has the resources to dramatically raise teacher pay in the current economy. However, the case study school began to celebrate small successes in other ways with the staff, and the staff began to respond positively. Small victory celebrations included cakes, pizza, certificates, and recognition—both with the school and in front of the school board/community. Local newspapers were fed prewritten stories for publication celebrating teachers and their work with students. Every small victory in student data was communicated and celebrated appropriately. When administrators praised the students in assemblies, they also praised the teachers who helped those students succeed.

As with students, a small "taste" of success can make a teacher crave more. Consider the case of the teacher who focused on state career technical standards for the first time last year. This list of standards became the focus of instruction, and lessons were designed around mastery of this set of standards. At the end of the year, student success rates on career measures in that technical teacher's content area rose from a previous 4 percent success rate to 39 percent—almost a tenfold increase in success rate. This year, *very few* lessons in that teacher's plans do not intentionally address a specific standard in some measurable way. Success leads to more success—if recognized and celebrated appropriately—just like it does with our students.

Strategy 29: Teacher Ownership of Professional Development—Explanation

Another way that student successes were celebrated and teacher professionalism was respected was the gradual release of professional development (PD) choices to the teachers themselves. In the case study school, teacher PD had often been structured as a whole-group, one-size-fits-all approach whereby every high school teacher received the same training regardless of content taught, years of experience, or skill level. This group PD was much easier to plan and usually cost less to the school because one "presenter" was cheaper than multiple sessions. However, this approach offered little to no opportunity for specialization and differentiation of the adult learning.

In the case study school, student performance drove the teachers' professional development plans. If a teacher's students showed proficiency in an area, that teacher was allowed to train in other areas of greater need. Often, a role model teacher with a specific skill set was paired with a teacher who needed to grow in that skill area for peer observation and reflection—leading to improved performance for both teachers.

Another way success was celebrated in the case study school was by the teacher *expert* program. The administrators purchased a variety of engaging education books, covering a wide variety of school improvement ideas and initiatives (for example, standards-based learning, working with difficult students, parents as partners in learning). Based on the teacher's personal growth plan and classroom data trends, each teacher received a specific book to read and reflect on. The teachers were allowed to count this reading and reflection as six hours of paid professional development and could accomplish this task on their own schedule.

Each teacher created a short summary of key points from their reading to share with the rest of the staff. This development led to reflective growth in many different areas by the staff. The administrators developed and published a list of "experts" in each area that other staff could ask for advice.

This increase in flexibility of PD for staff was viewed as a reward for improved student achievement and as a validation of their professional success. The level of professional conversation continued to rise in the case study school, and teachers continued to develop their skill levels with the goal of increasing student achievement.

School Culture Self-Assessment

1. Does your school foster a "culture of care" that can be felt all over the building and by all who work (and study) in your school every day?
2. Does your school's principal model servant leadership?

3. Is school leadership more people focused or more focused on an assembly line model?
4. Does school leadership model and provide training on how to effectively communicate and relate to others (emotional intelligence)?
5. Are students in your school experiencing a more growth-oriented mindset or a more fixed mindset?
6. Do teachers in your school embrace project-based learning and other nontraditional learning strategies that give more ownership to the student?
7. Do teachers in your school celebrate state-of-the-art instructional technology being utilized by students in the classroom?
8. Do you experience joy at work as a routine part of your daily and weekly life as a teacher?
9. Are students in your school offered an array of curricular, co-curricular, and extracurricular options? What do they share on student surveys about the school's total menu of services?
10. Does your school utilize a customized student interview process or do you rely only on a state-mandated tool?
11. Is your school culture one of trust, relationship, community, and celebration?
12. Do you as a teacher in this school feel empowered and equipped to transform your classroom to a more effective student-centered model?

Conclusion

The research and development of the strategies and processes contained within *Student Ownership* occurred over an extended period of time. Some of them will work well in other settings. Others may only work in our unique case study rural high school. Only through implementation and modification will you find those pieces that are useful for your particular faculty and your particular students.

In order for these strategies to be effective, the teachers must convince the students (and themselves) that college and career readiness is important for all students and that CCR is a reachable goal for all regardless of perceived skill level or any other academic barrier. Teachers must agree that

   i. the kids are not broken,
  ii. regardless of what they say, all students want to be successful, and
 iii. early success leads to later success.

The strategies and activities contained within this module help students own their learning and help teachers establish a sustainable culture of college and career readiness excellence for all students.

Establish a VISION
Enable OWNERSHIP
Embed MONITORING
Enact INTERVENTION
Empower CELEBRATION

References

Dufour, R., R. Dufour, R. Eaker, and T. Many. 2006. *Learning by Doing: A Handbook for Professional Learning Communities at Work.* Bloomington, IN: Solution Tree Press.

Muhammad, A. 2009. *Transforming School Culture: How to Overcome Staff Division.* Bloomington, IN: Solution Tree Press.

Payne, R. 1998. *A Framework for Understanding Poverty.* Baytown, TX: RFT Publishing.

Stiggins, R., J. Arter, J. Chappuis, and S. Chappuis. 2006. *Classroom Assessment for Student Learning.* Portland, OR: Educational Testing Service.

Willian, L. 2014. "Implementation of a Student Centered Approach: Impacting School Culture and College/Career Readiness." Unpublished doctoral dissertation, Morehead State University, Morehead, Kentucky.

Recommendations for Further Reading

Arbinger Institute. 2015. *Anatomy of Peace.* San Francisco: Berrett-Koehler.

Ashkenas, R., D. Ulrich, T. Jick, and S. Kerr. 2002. *The Boundaryless Organization.* San Francisco: Jossey-Bass.

Bakke, D. 2005. *Joy at Work.* Seattle: PVG.

Blanchard, K. 2007. *Leading at a Higher Level.* Upper Saddle River, NJ: Prentice Hall.

Block, P. 2009. *Community.* San Francisco: Berrett-Koehler.

Bolman, L. G., and T. E. Deal. 1995. *Leading with Soul.* San Francisco: Jossey-Bass.

Cloud, H. 2010. *Necessary Endings.* New York: Harper Business.

Covey, S. R. 2004. *The 8th Habit.* New York: Free Press.

Dweck, C. S. 2016. *Mindset—The New Psychology of Success.* New York: Ballantine Books.

Finzel, H. 1998. *Empowered Leaders.* Nashville, TN: W Publishing Group.

Fullan, M. 2003. *The Moral Imperative of School Leadership.* Thousand Oaks, CA: Corwin Press.

Gladwell, M. 2002. *The Tipping Point.* New York: Little, Brown.

Goleman, D., R. Boyatziz, and A. McKee. 2002. *Primal Leadership.* Boston: Harvard Business School Press.

Greenleaf, R. K. 1977. *Servant Leadership.* Mahwah, NJ: Paulist Press.

Huling, J., C. McChesney, and S. Covey. 2012. *The 4 Disciplines of Execution.* New York: Free Press.

Jennings, K., and J. Stahl-Wert. 2003. *The Serving Leader.* San Francisco: Berrett-Koehler.

Maxwell, J. C. 2010. *Everyone Communicates Few Connect.* Nashville, TN: Thomas Nelson.

Maxwell, J. C. 2007. *Talent Is Never Enough.* Nashville, TN: Thomas Nelson.

Murphy, J., and D. Torre. 2014. *Creating Productive Cultures in Schools for Students, Teachers, and Parents.* Thousand Oaks, CA: Corwin Press.

Palmer, P. J. 2007. *The Courage to Teach.* San Francisco: John Wiley.

Pfeffer, J. 1998. *The Human Equation.* Boston: Harvard Business School Press.

Professional Standards for Educational Leaders. 2015. Reston, VA: National Policy Board for Educational Administration.

Robinson, K. 2015. *Creative Schools.* New York: Penguin Books.

Sergiovanni, T. J. 2005. *Strengthening the Heartbeat.* San Francisco: Jossey-Bass.

About the Authors

Lewis Willian is a former administrator in Kentucky's P–12 system. During his thirty-year career, he spent five years on loan to the Kentucky Department of Education as a school turnaround agent and principal coach, serving in four of the lowest performing schools in the state. Each of the schools he served made remarkable progress, each exiting the persistently low achieving status during and after his tenure. He earned his doctorate in educational leadership from Morehead State University in 2014.

Lewis serves as an assistant professor in the school of education at Asbury University. His major teaching load is in the postmasters' principal licensure program. He also serves as a mentor and guide for practicing principals across the state. This is his first book. His retired (educator) wife of thirty-three years, Carol, is a children's minister at Central Baptist Church in Winchester, Kentucky. Son Matt (wife Ashley) and daughter Julie (husband Jonathan) are active in serving their congregations and communities in the areas where they live. Most importantly, grandkids Eli (four), Ella (two), and Annie (six months) love their Pop!

Rocky Wallace is a former administrator in Kentucky's P–12 system and has served at the Kentucky Department of Education as a leadership consultant to school principals. While principal at Catlettsburg Elementary in Boyd County, the school was named a Kentucky and U.S. Blue Ribbon School (1996–1997). Wallace has also served as the director of instructional support at the Kentucky Educational Development Corporation (KEDC) and earned his doctorate in strategic leadership from Regent University in 2007.

Rocky came to Asbury from Morehead State University and coordinates Asbury's principal licensure/EDS degree program, while also teaching and designing graduate educational leadership courses and developing various projects with P–12 partners. Rocky has written a series of four books on school improvement and the effectiveness of the servant leadership model and has also co-authored three other books on school culture. His wife, Denise, is a graduate of Asbury Theological Seminary, and the two co-pastor Carlisle United Methodist Church in Nicholas County, Kentucky. Their daughters, Lauren (husband Ely) and Bethany (husband Troy), and granddaughter Corrie Brooke are graduates of Asbury University.

Made in the USA
Monee, IL
04 June 2021